A CHRISTIAN PERSPECTIVE ON POP CULTURE

SCOTT MONCRIEFF

REVIEW AND HERALD® PUBLISHING ASSOCIATION

Since 1861 | www.reviewandherald.com

Published by Review and Herald® Publishing Association, Hagerstown, MD 21741-1119

Review and Herald® titles may be purchased in bulk for educational, business, fund-raising, or sales promotional use. For information, please e-mail SpecialMarkets@reviewandherald.com.

The Review and Herald® Publishing Association publishes biblically based materials for spiritual, physical, and mental growth and Christian discipleship.

The author assumes full responsibility for the accuracy of all facts and quotations as cited in this book.

Unless otherwise noted, Scripture quotations are from the *New American Standard Bible,* Copyright © 1960, 1962, 1963, 1968, 1971, 1972, 1973, 1975, 1977, 1994 by The Lockman Foundation. Used by permission.

Texts credited to Message are from *The Message.* Copyright © 1993, 1994, 1995, 1996, 2000, 2001. Used by permission of NavPress Publishing Group.

Texts credited to NIV are from the *Holy Bible, New International Version.* Copyright © 1973, 1978, 1984, International Bible Society. Used by permission of Zondervan Bible Publishers.

This book was
Edited by Penny Estes Wheeler
Copyedited by Lori Peckham
Designed by Trent Truman
Cover art by iStockphoto
Interior design by Heather Rogers
Typeset: News Gothic 10/14

PRINTED IN U.S.A.

11 10 09 08 07   5 4 3 2 1

Library of Congress Cataloging-in-Publication Data
Moncrieff, Scott, 1959-
  Screen deep : a Christian perspective on pop culture / Scott Moncrieff.
    p. cm.
  1. Popular culture–Religious aspects–Christianity. I. Title.
  BR115.C8M645 2007
  261–dc22
                              2007023200

ISBN 978-0-8280-2066-4

Dedication

To my parents,
Robert and Jacqueline Moncrieff,
who more than held up their end of the bargain.

Acknowledgment

Some of these pieces appeared previously
in slightly different forms on the *Spectrum* Web site
(www.spectrummagazine.org), in *Spectrum,* and
in the *Adventist Review*. Many thanks to the editors of
those magazines for their encouragement and interest,
and to the editors of this current project. Writers
generally have to imagine their readers, but editors
give us a living, breathing, book-loving
sounding board. We appreciate your efforts.

Thanks to my writing teachers throughout
the years. Your love for language inspired me—and even if I
dissed it in your class, I really like "The Red Wheelbarrow" now.

Also, in preparing the book, I was considerably
aided by some fine Bible study-oriented Web sites,
most notably www.biblegateway.com.

And to Lilia—far above rubies.

Contents

Introduction:
The Gold Standard

The gold standard, traditionally, is an economic system in which paper currency stands for a certain amount of gold. Paper is used because it's easier to carry around and divide, but the paper is backed up by gold. From that usage, however, the term has come to mean that which sets the standard, or supreme level of quality, in any particular field or endeavor.

Tiger Woods has set the gold standard in the world of golf (*USA Today*). The New England Patriots are (or were) the gold standard of the NFL. Vinyl is still the gold standard of recorded music (www.msnbc.com). Hildegarde, "The Dear That Made Milwaukee Famous," set a gold standard for singers (the Milwaukee *Journal Sentinel*). Ed Bradley set the gold standard of journalism (Los Angeles *Times*), which was earlier set by Edward R. Murrow (www.amazon.com). Wait a second—by definition, there can be only one gold standard per field. The term gets devalued when we apply it to any notable human achievement.

There is a gold standard, though, that deserves the name. When Jesus finished the Sermon on the Mount, we are told, the crowd was "astonished" or "amazed" at His teaching (Matthew 7:28). *The Message* translation says "the crowd burst into applause." It is an amazing sermon, and Matthew puts his finger on the reason: "because [Jesus] taught as one who had authority, and not as their teachers of the law" (verse 29, NIV). It stands to reason that the Creator of this world would have special insight into human problems and their solutions, and Christians identify the teachings of Jesus, and the Bible as a whole, as the gold standard for evaluating the truth of the human condition and the purpose of life.

At Jesus' time and in ours, however, there are different models for interpreting the world and setting values and priorities, and we get much of the information by which we do this from popular culture. According to a study by the Kaiser Family Foundation (2005), the average young person (8 to 18 years old) spends an average of six and one half hours per day using media; with watching TV, videos, or DVDs at just under four hours per day (3:51), followed by listening to music (1:44), using the computer (1:02), playing video games (:49), reading (:43), and watching movies in a theater (:25). That's nearly a full workday, just spent on media.

The very fact that you are reading this book suggests that you're not at the high end of the music and video spectrum for media consumption. If you were, I would encourage you to start playing table tennis or visiting nursing homes or learning how to operate a jackhammer—anything to increase your sensitivity to the real world. Since that's not you, however, I'll share a second concern: that you could improve on your critical-thinking skills in relation to media consumption. It's easy to drift into the relax-and-be-entertained mode when a DVD starts up or when one Web site after another flashes on the screen. We suspend thinking and passively respond to the manipulation of the source.

The aim of this book is to engage popular culture with critical thinking; critical thinking that draws its gold standard from biblical truth. The apostle Paul exhorts us to "examine everything carefully" and then "hold fast to that which is good" (1 Thessalonians 5:21), and that's what I'll be trying to do as I look with you at a number of reference points from popular culture.

I should note, however, that although for humans the gold standard is a real scale of value, God operates at an even higher plane. Gold, according to the travel brochure in Revelation, is going to be used for pavement in heaven (Revelation 21:21), and David appreciates God's judgments as being "more precious than gold, than much pure gold" (Psalm 19:10, NIV). We need to be continuously calibrating our human values (as we see exhibited plentifully in popular culture) against God's measuring stick, where even the gold standard falls short.

Passages to consider: *Psalm 119:1, 2; Acts 17:11.*

PART 1: TV

Lost

The cast, season 1:
Jack Shephard (Matthew Fox), spinal surgeon
Kate Austen (Evangeline Lilly)
James "Sawyer" Ford (Josh Holloway)
Shannon Rutherford (Maggie Grace)
Boone Carlyle (Ian Somerhalder)
Sun Kwon (Yunjin Kim)
Jin Kwon (Daniel Dae Kim)
Walter "Walt" Lloyd (Malcolm David Kelley)
Michael Dawson (Harold Perrineau, Jr.)
John Locke (Terry O'Quinn)
Sayid Jarrah (Naveen Andrews)
Hugo "Hurley" Reyes (Jorge Garcia)
Claire Littleton (Emilie de Ravin)
Charlie Pace (Dominic Monaghan)

The popular TV series *Lost* depicts the lives of the surviving passengers of a plane crash. The plane, en route from Sydney to Los Angeles, veers off course and deposits the passengers—most of whom escape the crash with unexplainably minor injuries—on a mysterious island. They are indeed lost, as they cannot determine where they are, nor can they communicate with the outside world. They are on their own and must create a new society, borrowing rules and ideas from the place they left, but also adapting to their new environment and multicultural mix. Although the show is obviously a commercial venture, an entertainment package, it

16

is also a forum for raising interesting questions about the nature and meaning of human existence. One of the first questions has to do with the concept of being lost itself.

1. Being Lost

Every now and again when I'm out jogging, a car pulls up beside me, and the driver rolls down the window. "Can you tell me how to get to Buchanan?" or "How do you get to Tabor Hill Winery?" or "How do you get to Three Oaks?" I enjoy giving directions. It's reassuring to know where you are and how to get from one place to another. I have a mental map of all the main roads in my area—lately upgraded by aerial images from Google Earth—and I know right where I fit within the grid. My location, and my sense of where I fit in relation to everything else, is part of my identity.

My name is also part of my identity. If, in a crowded airport terminal, someone hollers "Scott," I snap my head around. My work is key to my identity. From my Nethery Hall window, I look out on the Andrews University campus, watch the morning sun pour over Johnson Gym into the big oak tree at the sidewalk junction, and know I'm at home. I walk into classroom 205 upstairs, see the squirrels chasing each other through the branches outside the window, hear the heaters crackling, and know where I am.

The people around me contain part of my identity. I wake up beside my wife and have reflected back to me my married identity. I take the check with our son's tuition money to the business office and feel my parent identity. I pass this or that colleague or student in the hall and feel my work identity. All these things—sense of location, name, work, familiar persons—help create who I am, the parameters within which I function. The characters on *Lost* lose all that—or at least parts of all that.

They don't know where they are. And unlike the drivers I talk to, they have no easy way to get back on the main road. They have lost their jobs, although several of them find ways to adapt their former skills and services to island life. They have lost familiar relationships and must form new ones on the island. Some of them even lose their names—that is, they operate under aliases, assumed identities. They are lost, cut off.

But there is one more very important sense in which many of them are lost. All the main characters have highly developed back stories—histories that precede the crash—and they must come to terms with their past circumstances and choices while on the island. These are airline passengers with lots of excess personal baggage.

Charlie, for instance, is a heroin addict, and in addition to the physiological problems this creates, he has a bad history of personal relationships tied into his drug usage. Jack had serious relationship problems with his alcoholic father. Sawyer is a con artist, living under an assumed name, with a troubled past. Claire is an unwed mother-to-be who had planned to give up her baby for adoption. Shannon and Boone have serious relationship problems. Sayid worked for the Republican Guard during the Gulf War and "had" to torture the people he was interrogating. Kate has too many problems to mention in a short book. In short, each of these characters has major unresolved issues from their past that affect their ability to function productively in the present. Personally, they are lost.

This brings us around to the Christian sense of being lost, which might be described as being out of contact with God. If the North Pole and the lines of latitude and longitude create our geographical orientation on planet Earth, our relationship to God creates our spiritual orientation: He is our North Pole, and if we are not lined up with His will, we are not lined up with reality and are, in the most profound sense, lost.

The trouble is that the characters of *Lost* try to find themselves rather than to find God, as any presentation of the biblical God would be far too fundamentalist for mainstream television. Thus they put temporary bandages over old wounds and feel better for a time. Shannon's relationship with Sayid gives her relief from her problems with Boone and helps her self-confidence—but when Boone dies, she has a fit of vengefulness. Jack enjoys a friendship with Kate—until he finds out that he can't trust her. Charlie, with the help of Locke, overcomes his drug habit—but then he finds some more drugs on the island, and his temptations begin all over again.

Without God as a point of orientation and a supplier of grace—and with episode writers who always need new sources of conflict—the characters are doomed to a one-step-forward-two-steps-backward rhythm. After a dozen episodes, this trial and error cycle gets incredibly depressing, because—headline!—it doesn't have to be this way.

Yes, Christians are definitely subject to temptation, setbacks, and failure, but we can turn to God in every trial, and that makes an incredible difference. When I see these characters' lives, I think what a difference forgiveness (the kind we can get only from God) and grace could make for them. Instead of continually running on the old hamster's wheel that the devil loves to keep spinning, they could get off the island!

As I said, the unwritten rules of prime-time television don't allow the characters to turn to God in any serious way, but that's no restriction on us. And fortunately, God has made it His special business to find those who are lost and to help them get back on track. But just like the drivers I meet, we have to be willing to stop and ask directions—from Someone who really knows the way—and then follow them.

Passage to consider: *Matthew 18:11, 12.*

2. Relationships Rule

One of the most interesting things about *Lost* is the focus on relationships. When I was growing up, the relationships on TV tended to be pretty superficial and arranged for laughs: Barney Fife and Andy Griffith, Wilbur and Mister Ed, Dennis the Menace and Mr. Wilson, Hogan and Colonel Klink. As a serious drama with some very good writers, *Lost* deals with much more complex relationships, often with subtlety and insight.

Sawyer is a misanthrope, but not altogether. Kate understands more of him than anyone, but there's still a mystery about him. Kate has a very troubled past and combines toughness with vulnerability, compassion with calculation. She relates strongly with both Jack and Sawyer, who each seem to understand different sides of her. Charlie and Claire form a complex relationship, as do Sayid and Shannon. Boone latches on to Locke, while Walt and his father, Michael, try to work up a bond after years of separation.

Each character longs for friendship with certain others, longs to feel connected, but in each case there are obstacles to a good relationship from the character's past. Sawyer has a strong self-hatred for becoming like the man who seduced his mother. Jack has a tough time coming to terms with a demanding and alcoholic father. Charlie's drug dependence has left a trail of broken relationships. And the list could go on, character by character.

In portraying a series of broken relationships pitted against a longing for connectedness, *Lost* is not just creating interesting television drama. It shows our fallen human condition pitted against an inborn longing for the original design that God had for us. However, within the confines of prime-time TV, Lost is not going to go to the Bible and a restored relationship with God as the spring from which enduring and noble human friendships flow. Instead, it comes up with partway solutions, good in so far as they go, but only part of the solution.

In the episode "The Moth," we watch as Charlie, with Locke's help, is able to choose to give up his drug addiction. By having Kate know his dark secrets and still care about him, Sawyer is able to become a bit less misanthropic. Through a talk with Sawyer, Jack finds out that his father, at the end of his life, expressed strong and sincere appreciation for his son. All these efforts at the human level are meaningful and helpful, but as I said before, mere human efforts can't cut it in creating the high level of friendships that God intends for us. For that we need His grace, His forgiveness, the leading of His Spirit.

For example, in my relationship with my wife, certain human techniques, if you will, are very helpful. If I make a conscious effort to immediately spend time with her when I come home at the end of a workday, ask her how her day has gone, and see what's on her mind, the rest of the evening goes much better than if I walk straight to my bass for practice. And if she does something that irritates me—let's say I'm starving and supper isn't ready at 6:00 p.m.—I have found that it's best not to open my big mouth. If I step back and think about our relationship in its broader context, these are minor details and hardly worth mentioning. So a few conscious good habits can be very helpful.

However, beyond good technique or habits, my relationship to God has an extreme impact on my relations with human beings, and this is something that doesn't appear in Lost. Realizing that God has forgiven me, that He has given His life for me, plays a crucial role in helping me be accepting of others who may wound me. Knowing that God longs to pour His love into me gives me a vital resource when I feel my human love coming up short. Knowing that God created humans to give each other companionship and that He longs to use His Spirit to build community gives me courage, even when I see bitterness or cynicism around me.

One thing I noticed in watching a season of Lost is that the relationships are very volatile. Jack and Kate can be building a bond of trust at one moment—as when, in the pilot for season 1, Kate sews up the wound on

Jack's back—and then immediately drops into distrust—as when Jack finds out that Kate was being returned to the U.S. as a prisoner.

It might be argued that this volatility makes the relationships interesting, good television. This is partly true but misses the point that in real life a solid relationship is much, much more satisfying. I might go crazy if I drove home every night wondering if my wife and kids would like me, or if any whim or turn of events could turn them against me (or me against them). That's not the way God intended our relationships to be. And that's not the way they will be when we try to live in accordance with His will and ask Him to help us relate to others. True, we can't control other people's actions, but as we become more stable in His love, we create that much more potential for stability in all our relationships.

Lost shows us that relationships with other human beings are one of the most important things in giving life value. God shows us how to make these relationships as good as they can be.

Passage to consider: *1 Corinthians 13.*

3. The Greater Good

One of the more interesting episodes of *Lost* is titled "The Greater Good." It features Sayid being pressured by U.S. and Australian intelligence operatives into going undercover and joining an Islamic terrorist organization in Australia in order to secure some missing explosives, as well as to track the ringleaders of the organization. Sayid finds the plan distasteful and says no, but then the intelligence agents turn the screws on him by saying that they will reunite him with a woman he loves, and has been looking for, if he will perform this operation. He agrees.

Sayid has been chosen for the job because he has a former friend in the particular terrorist cell in question. And when Sayid presents himself at a local mosque (in Sydney), he "bumps into" the friend, and their old relationship is rekindled. Sayid is faced with the moral repugnance of imposing on his friend, pretending to be acting from friendship rather than his real motives, in order to win the chance to see the woman he loves. (If you've had an old friend pressuring you to buy something they're selling, you feel the tension.)

It gets worse. His friend is chosen to perform a suicide bombing, and being of a tender nature and horror-struck at the thought of killing innocent people, he balks. Sayid also wants out, but in come the intelligence operatives telling Sayid that he must go forward if they are to save innocent lives. In fact, they insist, Sayid must convince his friend to go through with the suicide bombing. He must insist that it's OK to kill these innocent people "for the greater good" of their radical cause. Sayid must argue a morality he himself has renounced.

In flashbacks, in this episode and others, we are shown that Sayid formerly tortured prisoners of the Iraqi regime in order to find out information that was vital to the state. He was not a sadist and did not enjoy the torture by any means, but he submitted to using it because he believed that it was "for the greater good." When, in an earlier episode, Sayid suggests torturing Sawyer in order to get him to give up an inhaler for asthmatic Shannon, Sayid becomes disgusted with himself for reverting to ways he had renounced. Both Sayid and the viewers, in the episode that includes torturing Sawyer, come to a clear realization that "good" cannot use evil means to achieve good, or it no longer is good.

In "The Greater Good," Sayid finally convinces his friend to blow himself up, thus killing innocent bystanders, but only by agreeing to complete the martyr's mission with him. However, at the last moment, Sayid stops the plan and tells his friend to flee before the CIA show up to arrest him. The friend, realizing the betrayal—that Sayid had set him up—loses his mental balance and shoots himself. Sayid will now be told where his old girlfriend is, but at what a cost: he, even though coerced, was instrumental in the suicide of his old friend. Such is the result, in this case, of using bad means to a good end.

The whole question of means and end is vital to God. Satan has made dangerous charges about God's character. God must defend Himself. Should God wipe out Satan and erase the affected angels' memories in order to clear the record and start over? That would be the quick and easy way, and if anyone would be justified in doing such a thing, it would be God.

Instead, God undertakes a much longer, more painful process, but one that carefully protects human free will. In a classic experiment God allows Satan's way and its results to be carried out, within limitations, and demonstrates His way side by side. While performing the experiment, He doesn't cook the books, but does everything with an open hand, so that those of us who are interested can observe closely and make up our own minds as to the results. Although Satan constantly uses unfair means and lies, God refrains—the means themselves are part of the end. His fairness and character of love are the very things that are on trial, and He will not use means that contradict His character.

His willingness to have His beloved Son come to earth and live and die among people He created shows us the length to which God is willing to go to play fair. God is always thinking of "the greater good," and vital to that greater good is doing nothing to compromise it by evil means.

Lost sometimes suggests that characters are compelled to do wicked things to achieve good results—as when Michael is "forced" to betray a party of his friends in order to be reunited with Walt, a major plot angle of season 2. God doesn't work that way—for Him, there is no moral separation of means and end. I take that to mean that there shouldn't be any such separation for us, either.

Passages to consider: *Proverbs 16:25; Hebrews 6:18.*

4. It's a Material World

When I read *Walden* in a college American lit class, I was profoundly moved by Thoreau's doctrine of simplicity (see my section called "C28 Clothing"). Since that time, I have shared the American ambivalence toward the choice between returning to nature and loading up with the latest material goods. For instance, I wouldn't mind driving an eco-friendly Prius (would Thoreau drive a Prius?), but unless this book generates an unforeseen amount of royalties, I will likely be chugging along in my '94 Honda for a few more years. (Thoreau would probably stick with walking.)

Lost plays both sides of the fence. On the one hand, we enjoy seeing the islanders catch their own food and make do with simple shelters and limited clothing. Because material goods themselves, as well as the pursuit of them, frequently lead to a kind of slavery, we enjoy the primitive simplicity of the *Lost* characters' material lives—it feeds our inner Thoreau.

However, in addition to the few material goods the passengers salvaged from the crash, in just about every show *Lost* jumps to flashbacks of material opulence: Sawyer and his briefcase full of money; nice suits; new cars; lavish hotels—all things that we associate with material luxuriance. Not to mention the commercials—more than 15 minutes' worth on the hour—pushing everything from soft drinks to SUVs.

For a Christian in a developed country, dealing with material goods, standing strong against the onslaught of consumerist propaganda that is always telling us we need more, deciding when enough is enough—these are some of the great challenges of contemporary life. Every day our spiritual development and our "big picture" perspective on life is threatened by having too much.

I like reading *Consumer Reports*. I like how the magazine's writers lay out testing criteria for sports cars, HDTVs, microwaves, or whatever, and write up the results. However, in recent years I've realized that sometimes I use carefully researching a product as sufficient justification to buy it. After all, if I've compared the different lawn mowers, am I not acting as a responsible Christian with my money when I buy the top-rated Grassalator 9000? What I forgot, in the midst of my careful research, was that if I got a $50 tune-up on our 7-year-old Weed Wimp 150, we could still do a perfectly adequate job for our lawn.

Jesus reminds us to "Beware, and be on your guard against every form of greed; for not even when one has an abundance does his life consist of his possessions" (Luke 12:15). The parable of the sower calls attention to the seed that falls among thorns, representing potential believers who are too much concerned with the "worries of this life, the deceitfulness of wealth and the desires for other things" (Mark 4:19, NIV), which "choke the word, making it unfruitful." We should not imagine that these warnings apply only to the Donald Trump and Bill Gates types of this world. Pretty much everyone living in a developed country has enough material goods to constitute a potential briar patch, and only by daily asking God to help us sort out the truly important from the clutter can we have room in our lives for the fruit God longs to produce in us. For *Lost*, lack of material goods is part of creating an interesting alternative reality to entertain glutted viewers; for you and me, a proper perspective on material goods clears the way for God to do some serious farming.

Passages to consider: Consider the story of Solomon, who decided to gratify himself with every material possession and found it all to be vanity (Ecclesiastes 2). I talk about this passage in the "Hogan" section. See also Luke 14:33.

5. A Second Chance
(the Grace of Lost and Grace of God)

One of the prevalent theories about the metaphysical meaning behind *Lost* is that the characters are in a sort of purgatory, presented with a chance to redeem themselves from the misdeeds of their previous lives. Thus, Jin might redeem himself from being a Japanese gangster, Sawyer from being a hustler, Michael from being an absent father, Charlie from being an addict and doing bad things to support his drug habit.

My theory is a little different: that the metaphysical meaning behind *Lost* is to write a successful TV show and keep it going as long as possible, and if throwing in a hodgepodge of spiritual concepts from incompatible belief systems will boost ratings, the writers are glad to oblige. In other words, the writers are happy to dabble in Christian concepts, Darwinian concepts, Eastern religious concepts, and whatever else they can use—without committing to any of them. That way, the viewers who line up with each orientation can find something to identify with. The other perspectives are not presented as ultimate truth either, but just possibilities, so everyone is (sort of) happy.

We can see this hodgepodge approach to the purgatory or second-chance perspective as it pertains to Charlie in the first season's episodes 6 and 7, "The House of the Rising Sun" and "The Moth." Overall, these episodes present Locke's attempt to help Charlie through withdrawal from drug addiction, and to show Charlie transforming from one who would do any act to get drugs to one who will deliberately reject drugs when they are offered.

In episode 6 Locke suggests to Charlie that the island is a sort of testing ground, and if Charlie will be willing to give up his small remaining stash of drugs, the island just might give him his guitar, which he has not recovered from the crash. When Charlie hands over the goods, Locke tells him to look up. "You're not going to ask me to pray or something?" asks Charlie. No, Locke is just pointing up the cliff to where Charlie's guitar case miraculously hangs intact, supported by roots and vines creeping down the side of the cliff. It's a good example of the "natural supernaturalism" the show employs, in which a greater purpose and directing hand is hinted at, while simultaneously a rational explanation is provided.

In "The Moth" Charlie, suffering through withdrawal, asks for his drugs back. Locke tells him that he will return them if Charlie asks three times, and he has just spent "once." Right away, from a TV drama standpoint, you can be certain that he's going to ask for the drugs again, and then a couple of minutes before the end of the episode, as we are building to a climax, he'll ask the third time.

When Charlie asks the second time, right on schedule, halfway through the show, Locke tells him the parable of the moth. Pointing to a nearby cocoon, he tells Charlie that he could help the moth inside escape by widening the escape hole with his knife, but then the freshly liberated moth wouldn't have the strength (built up by struggling out of the cocoon) to survive. Chastened, Charlie backs down.

Meanwhile, Jack gets trapped in a cave-in, and only Charlie is small enough to crawl in after him. A subsequent cave-in traps Charlie with Jack, and they seem to be running out of air until Charlie spots a moth flying in the cave. Never mind that there is no light source, and inside the cave it would be pitch-dark. Guided by the moth, Charlie starts digging, and in a few minutes reaches the surface and finds an alternative escape route for Jack and himself.

Near the end of the show, Charlie approaches Locke and asks for his drugs a third time. Locke reluctantly complies, but then we experience a Hallmark moment as Charlie drops the drugs in the fire, signifying his release from addiction. Violin music rises as Charlie looks upward and beholds a moth fluttering up into the night sky.

Again, the idea of a supernatural hand behind Charlie's transformation is strongly suggested, but then again it could be just a coincidental moth. Locke, so strongly the man of faith in these early episodes, is later held in thrall by the hatch, and later by the computing system that has to be reset continually—in other words, by a bunch of goofy superstition. This illustrates one of the problems I have with *Lost*. It's a smart show. It has good writing, acting, cinematography, and it dabbles with interesting, potentially Christian concepts, but it has never really committed to anything but to keeping the show going. It's like marching around near the Jordan River and then back across the wilderness, then back to the Jordan again, but never crossing over. That's what it's like to be lost.

And what is Charlie's result? In the short term, it's definitely good. Free of drugs, he is able to form more stable relationships, able to be much less self-centered. But he has no relationship with God to ground him, nothing more than his own temporary success and some well-meaning friends. That's the problem with an ill-defined spiritual sense, a misty moth flying off into the night sky. There's nothing to build on.

Christianity offers much more: a chance to build a really solid relationship with a God you can get to know, not some "concept" behind the island, not some puff of black smoke (as confronts Eko in an episode of the second season), not a noise from a hidden source, but a loving person who reveals Himself in a book, a Friend who is always available for personal communication.

Passages to consider: *Psalm 91:1, 2; John 15:12-16.*

6. The Sense of an Ending
(God's Plot Versus the Plot of Lost)

To have a plot, you need tension and resolution. Tension can be created by conflict, in which, for instance, two characters are headed on a collision course. Or the conflict could be internal, in which a character has to decide between moving to Ohio to take over his father's tire company or staying with his dying mother in Oregon. Dumb example, but you get the point.

Tension can also be created by enigma: the raising of a problem that must be understood and solved. For instance, a character discovers an old box in an attic, and we cut to a commercial. We don't yet know what's in the old box, but by the laws of plot we know that something significant is in there, and that if we hang around another 45 minutes, we'll find out what. Conflict and enigma create turmoil inside us, which is satisfied when resolution comes. The former make us hungry, so to speak, and the latter satisfies our hunger.

The master narrative of the great controversy gives an excellent illustration of this. God and His Son get together and create this world, including male and female in the image of God. He gives the couple one restriction: don't eat from the tree of the knowledge of good and evil. Enigma: what will they do? Satan enters the picture, tempts Eve. Conflict. She falls. Adam falls. What will God do? Enigma. God has a plan to restore humanity. How will it work? Enigma. The woman's seed and Satan will be "forever" at odds. Conflict.

And so on and so on, until Christ dies on the cross (major resolution), Christ returns (major resolution), and He takes His faithful ones back to heaven. After the earth is remade, humanity is restored to earth in its Eden state (final resolution). This is the megaplot in which we are living.

In *Lost*, each episode has a title and a central conflict, plus subsidiary conflicts. Typically, the episode has a featured character and focuses on a present situation of that character juxtaposed with a series of flashbacks from that character's life, with the episode as a whole showing how the character's past has led to the present moment and helped create the person he or she is, but also implying that the past is not determinative—the character can make free choices in the present moment.

For instance, in the episode "In Translation," which focuses on Jin's past, we see that even though he has been coerced into becoming his father-in-law's hit man, it is still up to him to decide if he will try to talk with Sun and revive his tenderness toward her or stay in the hardened shell he has created in recent years.

In terms of enigma, we see Locke asking Claire to help him build a project by sawing pieces of bamboo. Claire and Locke talk away while they work, and Claire casually wonders what they are building. At one point she supposes it may be a kind of animal trap—some long struts support that prediction. Suddenly, when it's finished, Locke turns it over, and we realize that it's a cradle. Claire, unwittingly, has been helping to build a cradle for her unborn baby. It's one of the beautiful and inspired moments of the series.

However, I'm getting a bit lost myself, and what I really want to be saying is, do you notice how almost every time *Lost* breaks for commercials it does so at a moment of high tension or enigma, accompanied by banging kettledrums or the special tension musical cue? Remember the old term "cliff-hanger"? It referred to a novel in serial form that left a character hanging over a cliff at the end of an episode so the audience would rush out and buy the next installment to see what happened. In one *Lost* episode Jack is literally hanging over a cliff (on a vine) as we cut to commercial break.

What is true of cuts to commercials is true of episode endings as well. Old style TV dramas, such as *Perry Mason*, always ended with resolution. Before the penultimate commercial, the criminal would be nailed by Perry in court and would blurt out self-incriminating words validating Perry's brilliant theory. Cut to commercial. The final scene would feature Perry, Della (his secretary), and Paul Drake (his favorite private investigator) sharing a joke around the office. Order was restored; everyone could lighten up.

In *Lost*, however, episodes typically end with a combination of resolution and new enigmas or conflicts. For instance, at the end of the episode about the birth of Claire's baby, her baby is born healthy, and most of the castaways are crowded around Claire admiring the baby at the end of the episode. However, in the distance Shannon and Sayid approach, and Jack has to go off to tell Shannon that her brother Boone has died. This definitely mutes the joy at the birth of the baby, and sets the stage for a later episode in which Shannon tries to avenge herself on Locke, whom she thinks has maliciously caused Boone's death.

At the end of season 1, there's a huge mystery about what's inside the hatch. It was built up with little hints for several episodes, and even your average couch potato could see it coming. After a tension-filled hour finding and transporting dynamite to blow the resistant hatch cover off, it is finally blasted, and the season ends with the revelation that a long rung of steps leads down from the opening. Of course we can't see where the steps lead. Enigma. There has to be a strong hook to pull us into watching the first episode next season.

The point of all this discussion about plotting is this. God's big plot works toward a final and ultimately satisfying resolution. The plot of *Lost*, however, is by its nature opposed to resolution. As long as *Lost* is profitable, has good viewer ratings, and is able to keep the core actors reasonably happy, the show will stay on the air. It will perpetually entice us forward with the hint of resolutions—yes, we do find out what's at the bottom of the hatch in season 2—but it will replace each resolution with another enigma or conflict, so that we can never be fully satisfied. Indeed, after two, three, or five more seasons, *Lost* will come to an end and the characters will return to civilization, but that will inevitably come as a final failure of the show to sustain itself. The actors will move on with their lives, and 15 or 20 years later they'll get together for the *Lost Reunion Show*, which, if successful, will spawn *Reunion II*, by which time there will be about a billion channels to watch and a successful show will have 11 viewers.

In short, the method of a popular TV series is to artificially produce continual complications so that the viewer will always imaginatively believe that satisfaction is always around the next corner, and then make it one more corner after that. The mechanism of God, if it may be spoken of in that way, is to solve real conflicts with real solutions to bring a real resolution.

Passages that consider God's narrative: Genesis 1:1; Hebrews 12:2; Revelation 22:13.

7. The God of the Island

In the episode "White Rabbit" (season 1, episode 5), Locke asks a question about the island that thinking beings ask about our planet: "What if everything happens for a reason here?" Quite a bit of attention in Lost goes into the mystery of what the basic operating rules of the island are and what, for lack of a better term, might be called "the god of the island."

This would include finding answers to questions such as "What kinds of animals live there?" Boars, which we might expect, are there, but also polar bears, which don't make sense in a tropical climate. The polar bears are important as a threat, but even more important as being metaphysically suggestive. The anomaly of polar bears suggests that maybe this island doesn't operate by the normal rules of nature. They suggest (and certainly this is part of TV hype, not just moral and philosophical pondering by the writers of the show) that something is out there that we don't know about, and they tease us from episode to episode about what that might be.

The pilot episode, part 1, ends with the question "What would do that?" in reference to the carnage inflicted on the pilot (the person who flies the plane) by, presumably, some jungle superbeast. It couldn't be any known beast, certainly not a polar bear, because the pilot's body is deposited 20 or 30 feet up in a tree. Another early scene has the characters along the beach first hearing the weird noises of some unknown creature in the interior. The quality of the noises suggests a threat out of proportion with known sources of danger.

At first the characters are just worried about protecting themselves from whatever large animals might be out there. But not much time passes before there begins to be a sense that they're not just up against animalistic power, but that there is an intelligence of some sort governing the affairs of the island. This intelligence is most strongly indicated in two ways: in the seeming plan behind the lives of the characters as they unfold on the island, and in the mystery of the hatch, which stubbornly reposes in ambiguity throughout much of season 1, and begins to be investigated in season 2.

When Locke asks the question alluded to above, it is rhetorical for him. After all, he experienced a miracle in the crash, recovering the use of his paralyzed legs, and he sees a benevolent force governing the affairs of the islanders. Locke is by no means a Christian; his faith might be described as intense religious mysticism oriented toward an ambiguous source. He sees the trials of the island as designed tests to bring the people of the island to a higher plane of existence. This philosophy is apparent in Locke's work with Charlie in the episode "The Moth." Charlie, a drug addict, is almost out of his supply. Locke leads Charlie along through the power of saying no to his addiction,

It's not so important how the series eventually works out who, if anyone, is behind all the coincidences and incidents on the island: it could be a person, a computer, a superbeast, some kind of magical figure. It doesn't really matter, because it's a fictional show and doesn't determine reality. What is important, for our purposes here, is that most of the characters want to figure out the nature of the reality of the island. If they believe that there's a benevolent force looking out for them, they will accept difficulty in a different way than if they think things just happen. If they think that there's a malevolent force out there after them, then, well, that's not good, but at least they know how to act.

There's a huge to-do the whole second season about punching numbers into a computer, and whether the failure to do so will bring about the destruction of—those of you who haven't been watching, don't laugh too loud—the whole world. Our individual decisions about whether God exists or not and is benevolent or not have nothing to do with whether God actually exists and what His character is like. If He exists, He exists, whether we believe in Him or not, and if He is good, He is good, whether we think so or not. Our belief, however, has a lot to do with the framework within which we see our actions.

If we believe that God exists and is good, and wants to be our friend, then it leads us to the opportunity to respond to that existence and that love. If we believe that God reveals His character to us through the biblical record, then we can choose to respond by studying that record. If we believe that God sent us an example of life rightly lived in His Son, Jesus, then we have the opportunity to immerse ourselves in that life. If we believe that

Jesus offers us the Holy Spirit to lead us into truth, then we have the opportunity to petition the Holy Spirit for that special guidance.

In all these examples, the way we believe about reality has a direct impact on the choices we make, the actions we take. I have a mild interest in what hokey explanation the writers of *Lost* eventually reveal as the mind and plan behind the reality of the island. I have a compelling interest in knowing about the reality of God and the way He wants me to live.

Passages to consider: *Psalm 34:8; Judges 6-8.*

Thou Shalt Have No (American) Idols Before Me

I confess. Before starting work on this section I had never watched an episode of *American Idol,* although I had been aware of its existence. Several hours of *Idol* clips later, I'm still trying to understand what all the fuss is about.

True, the combination of pulsating music, a light show, screaming, arm-waving audience members, spinning cameras, and gushy hosts bypassed my cynic's armor for a few seconds, and I felt the hair on my neck start to stand up, but it lay down again pretty quickly.

I was left wondering why 20 or 30 million Americans would spend a perfectly good hour per week watching this show when they could be drying the dishes or tweezing their nose hairs. In the next few chapters I will share a few hypotheses and comments about what the Christian might learn from thinking about *American Idol.*

1. A Time of Judgment

For many viewers, the most exciting part of *American Idol* may not be the performances, but the judgments. Is this person going on or going down? Will Simon give one of his notorious put-downs, along the lines of "That's the kind of singing that makes nails on a blackboard melodious"? Or will Paula Abdul say something such as "I can see you going right to the top with your talent. Where have you been hiding?" And the contestant will just light up and glow.

Either way, there's a vicarious thrill for the viewer. If the contestant is blasted, we can let out a little shiver and say, "I'm glad it wasn't me." And if they go on, we can easily, so easily, see ourselves dancing a little jig with them, doing a touchdown celebration, hanging on the rim after a thunderous dunk. Nothing for the poor old human ego quite like being publicly celebrated.

33

But getting back to judgment. Remember, if you've been around a few years, how much attention the O. J. Simpson trial got back in 1995? With 133 days of televised coverage, and an estimated 91 percent of people who were watching television tuned to the verdict on October 3 (www.law.umkc.edu/faculty/projects/ftrials/Simpson/simpson.htm), Simpson probably received the most public judgment ever. And then in 1998 and 1999 we had drawn-out national attention given to President Clinton's affair with Monica Lewinsky, and the resulting impeachment proceedings. I'm afraid there's a (fallen) part of us that loves to know all the dirt about another human being. How many of us, in such a situation, give ourselves a pat on the back and say, "Well, I may not be perfect, but look at that poor excuse for a human being"?

It's interesting, in this context, to be reminded of Jesus' clear admonition to "judge not, that ye be not judged" (Matthew 7:1, KJV). If one looks carefully at this passage, and at other passages about judgment, one can see that there are at least two kinds of judgment. From the adjacent words about taking the beam out of one's own eye before removing the mote from your brother's, one can see that hypocritical judgment is being particularly singled out. Judgment that arises from a spirit of "I'm better than you" is not to be part of a Christian's thoughts, as all of us have sinned and fall short of the glory of God (Romans 3:23).

On the other hand, there is a righteous judgment that Christians are called to make (John 7:24), not for the purposes of condemning another; rather, this is "the humble, wise, and constructive discernment between good and evil for the sake of God and the benefit of others" (Peters, www.brfwitness.org/Articles/1994v29n5.htm). So which kind of judgment does American Idol elicit, particularly on the part of the viewer? And what is the effect of that judging pleasure on the character of the viewer?

True, American Idol celebrates talent, and it showcases some pretty good performers, but an important drawing card for the show is to exploit untalented performers for laughs. It's true that these contestants put themselves forward and are, in that sense, asking for it, but I don't think it's very healthy laughter when it comes at the expense of other people.

So much for watching other people being judged. What about when we are in a position of judging? To start with the easier side, we can be sure that giving genuine positive feedback ought to be done as often as is practical. I love to hear my wife say "I love you," and even "Thanks for emptying the garbage" is nice. These are affirming judgments. I appreciate it when students or colleagues give a genuine thank-you for something positive I have done for them. I ask myself, How much am I contributing to the lives of others by taking the opportunities for genuine affirmation that fall in my lap?

Negative judgment? That's a tough one, especially for me, a nonconfrontational person. Maybe the first key ought to be not making and certainly not proclaiming judgments when they're not called for. That step alone will save a lot of grief. However, as a parent, spouse, friend, and (especially) teacher, I am bound to make and share judgments. I try to remember to ask God for wisdom before I grade each stack of papers, not because I think God will then rubber-stamp my verdicts and all is well, but because He promises to give generously to those who ask for wisdom (James 1:5). Additionally, I try to present negative comments in a constructive way and with tact.

In *American Idol*, the judgments are occasionally helpful and constructive, and generally reasonable—meaning that the judges are qualified critics and I believe they vote according to their consciences—but are primarily packaged for entertainment value, meaning that suspense, sarcasm, and punch dictate the delivery. It's a game show, not a model of Christian virtues.

As a final thought on this topic, there's one judgment I long to hear, and I wish it equally for you. It will certainly be a result of God's saving grace, but also our choices. That is, upon meeting our Lord, having Him tell us "Well done, thou good and faithful servant . . . enter thou into the joy of thy lord" (Matthew 25: 21, KJV). "You're going to Hollywood!" will be nothing, absolutely nothing, compared with that.

2. What's Wrong With Idol Worship?

Is it just me, or is there something genuinely noteworthy in the fact that the second commandment forbids idol worship and America's number-one-rated television show is *American Idol?* This juxtaposition leads me to further questions, such as: Why did God forbid idol worship? Is watching *Idol* really comparable to idol worship? What is it about the show that viewers find so attractive? What potential harm is there in the show?

I think we can start by assuming two conditions. First, God wouldn't have warned against idol worship if it were not something inherently harmful to the human species. If we start with the assumption that God is all wise and all-loving, then we can conclude that God wouldn't ask us not to do something unless that thing would be bad for us. Each commandment, as has been often remarked, is as much a guideline for how humans ought to live as it is a limitation on what they ought not to do.

Second, it stands to reason that God would not have condemned idol worship if it were not going to be a temptation. We don't tell people "Be sure not to . . ." unless we think there's a possibility that they will. There would be no reason to have speed limits if the unfettered drivers of America would automatically restrain their Lexus to 25 miles per hour in school zones when children are present.

OK, so if we accept that worshipping idols is bad for us, can we ask why it is bad? Beginning with the Old Testament meaning of idol—an image created by humans to represent a deity and/or object of worship—it doesn't take a rocket scientist to see a major problem. Worshipping an idol is a major distortion of reality, treating an inanimate object as if it were God. God wants us to know and act according to the truth, so He says, "Don't mess with idols."

But even if worshipping an Old Testament idol is bad, is it really the same or sufficiently similar to describe watching *American Idol* as idol worship? I'm going for "yes" on this answer, and here's why. Note the striking similarity of the words "idol" and "idol" in each case. Coincidence? Oh, but you say, these are people, not graven images. Sorry. After watching the show's hairstylist talk about changing the contestants' looks, after listening to the makeup artist talk about gluing on the false eyelashes, after looking closely at Carrie Underwood's pancaked face in an interview and wondering what was underneath the porcelain layer, after watching the way the lighting crew creates supercharged atmosphere on the stage, I'd have to say that the performers are at best a cross between graven images and real people.

And what about that word "worshipping"? Is that really what we're doing with these self-proclaimed idols? That's a question for each individual to answer, but without going out on a limb I can say that the screaming, sign-carrying, swaying fans the cameras show us certainly seem to be worshipping their favorites. Even here, though, there's a subtle danger.

Having been at live tapings of some TV shows, I know how the producers labor to get the audience worked into a frenzy, or should I say a pseudofrenzy, for the brief moments when the camera sweeps across them. I assume that many of the "worshippers" are in their seemingly ecstatic states for only seconds at a time. Yes, there are undoubtedly some hard-core fans who scream at their television sets and dial in their votes from a dozen different phones, but probably there are more watchers who console themselves by saying, "Well, I like the show and all that, but I'm not a raving loonie like those people." By categorizing others as more extreme, we justify our own weaknesses.

But for all of us, the whole idea of true worship is seriously compromised by allegiance to idols. The object of worship is not worthy of worship in the true sense of the word—true whether it's William Hung or Elvis up there—and the method of worship suggests mindless fanaticism rather than lucid tribute.

One last thought on *Idol* worship. Isn't it interesting that one of the catch-phrases of the show is having aspiring contestants proclaim, "I'm Billy-Bob Johnson"—or whatever—"and I'm the next American Idol." The next. The next. That's the good old US of A. Why are we always looking for "the next"? Because in a consumer economy the current whatever isn't enough, and more sales can be generated only by a new and better—or at least different—product.

In brilliant contrast to the next American Idol, God is the same yesterday, today, and forever (Hebrews 8:13). He doesn't have to worry about coming up with a new look, a new style, ratings for a new season, a new gimmick. He's God. The more I think about "worship" on *American Idol*, the more sense the second commandment makes.

3. Star Dumb

"It's the American Dream, encapsulated in a television show," says *Idol* executive producer Nigel Lythgoe. "You can be flipping burgers one day, you can be serving coffee, cleaning bathrooms, and the next day be onstage with Stevie Wonder . . ." So what's wrong with stardom?

Lythgoe's assessment implies a job hierarchy, with flipping burgers and cleaning bathrooms on the bottom and singing next to Stevie Wonder at the top. Or, actually, being Stevie Wonder must be at the top, and since that job is taken, singing next to him onstage must be the top job with an opening.

The hierarchical model is the way we tend to think. Competition is a big deal in America, from who's going to win in the football playoffs to who can eat the most hot dogs in five minutes. *Idol* is a great example of a pyramidal competition, with estimates of 100,000 people trying out at the beginning of the season, and after months of competition taking off all the zeros until only the "1" is left.

The problem I have with stardom is that it creates an asymmetrical relationship that depends upon some members of the community being more highly valued than others. Can you have a star without fans? Not without twisting the standard meaning of the word. Which number is higher, the stars or the fans? Well, the fans, naturally. And the biggest star is the one who has the most fans. So the bigger the asymmetry, the more the "star" fits the definition of the word.

I don't have a problem with recognizing skill and excellence, but stardom goes well beyond that, to worshipping certain figures and treating them as a special class of human beings. That seems to be pretty unhealthy for them and for the rest of us. You can see some of God's thinking on the way community ought to relate in the following instances:

*Although even some Christians might disagree with me, I think it's pretty clear that God created the first two human beings to work in partnership, not hierarchy.

*When the children of Israel clamored for a king (the Old Testament version of a star), God told them that it wasn't a very good idea, and that putting a human being in that exalted position was asking for trouble on both sides (1 Samuel 8).

*Luke tells us that in the early church believers held material goods in common, and that no one suffered from need (Acts 4:32-35).

The parables of the good samaritan (Luke 10) and the rich man and Lazarus (Luke 16), the story of the rich young ruler (Luke 18), and the institution of foot washing (John 13), all emphasize how we are bound to each other in community, and each one needs to look out for the other. Stardom is headed in the opposite direction.

OK, to be honest, it's nice for a few seconds to think of thousands of people excitedly screaming our name, of dozens of girls (in my adolescent fantasies) throwing themselves at me. Perhaps that's why a friend and I broke into "Hound Dog" and some other Elvis hits at an academy party way back when. Note: No girls threw themselves at us.

But when you think about it, the star/fan relationship has got to rank near the bottom in quality, because it depends on distance, on neither party knowing the other very well. The idea that I'm special and you're not, or that you're special and I'm not—well, neither should be very appealing to a Christian. The idea that "everyone is special" is illogical if "special" means out of the ordinary—sort of like arguing that everyone can be taller than average—and sounds like the sappy beginning to a United Way commercial. But everyone *is* special in the sense that God created us individually, uniquely, with particular talents to bring to the table.

All the people in the parable were given talents, even if of different amounts, and all were needed. Furthermore, the use of those talents is to be for the service of the community, not self-aggrandizement. The Christian community is built around an ethic of service and the idea that everyone has something different and important to contribute. And stardom and fandom are headed in a different direction.

Passages to consider: *Philippians 2:1-8; John 15:13.*

4. A Sense of Calling

Another interesting feature of *American Idol* is watching the contestants talk about their sense of calling to be music idols: "This is something I was born to do"; "This is just the start for me"; "Singing is at the heart of who I am"; "It's the greatest feeling knowing that so many people are watching you"; "This is what I want to do for the rest of my life"; "I know this is my calling"; "America will know who I am"; "No one will ever forget that performance"; "Broadway, that's where I belong"; "I want this more than a whole bag of gummy bears, Simon; come on."

That whole thing about a sense of calling can lie pretty heavily on one's mind. I remember when I was a confused freshman, talking with a number of people about how they figured out what they wanted to do and how I should figure out the same. I tested the waters my first two years as a journalism major (mainly); a PE major (I liked sports); a business major (working with long columns of numbers was not for me); and a pre-med major (I got grossed out doing dissections in academy, but since I hailed from Loma Linda and my father was a physician, I had to at least take anatomy and physiology). I even thought about a religion major and talked with a local pastor about how you could tell if you were called. It turned out that he was in the process of changing from a pastor to a dentist.

After my sophomore year, I just couldn't see myself going forward in journalism or public relations, so I took a year out and worked through Taskforce as a boys' dean and intramural director. That helped me rule out working as a dean! The following summer I hit on the idea of becoming a professional golfer. This was not due to natural ability—I was a decent player but a long way from professional standards. But I liked walking, hitting a golf ball, and walking some more. I liked being outdoors, liked smelling the grass, liked watching the ball fly through the air. Is this a calling, or what?

Problem. For professional golfers, whether tour players or teachers, business happens every weekend. I realized that Sabbath observance, in any traditional form, was incompatible with being a golf pro, and immediately felt a strong sense of injustice. Having grown up in the medical culture of Loma Linda, I was used to seeing doctors and nurses working on Sabbath. Why should they be allowed to have a career with no Sabbath conflict and not me? What if I were "called" to be a golfer and my religion was a big fat roadblock? It just wasn't fair. I wondered whether God would accept having me worship on Monday or Tuesday, or if I could, say, qualify for the Masters, do well on Thursday and Friday, then have a rainout on Saturday, and collect the trophy after a double round on Sunday. When you have lots of time on your hands, it's amazing what scenarios you can come up with.

I decided I would have to give up Sabbath—but not God. I imagined the reaction of my parents. I knew Mom would start crying, and like most men I'm defenseless against that tactic, so I went to talk to my dad at his office. He listened quietly to my proposal—he was always a good listener—and then he said something along the lines of "Well, son, that's not what your mother or I would choose for you, but if that's what you want to do, you can go ahead and try it—we'll stick with you." Wow. That was a big deal for me.

Since then I've often thought about my conversation with my dad, and now that I have sons in the mid- and upper-teen years, I've asked myself what I would do in a parallel situation. First, I think, I would pray a lot, because in general we humans get ourselves in some pretty big messes when we depend on our own genius.

For me, though, I think my father did the right thing. If he had said something such as "We won't be having any Sabbathbreaker around our house," or "Come back when you get this nonsense out of your head," my natural inclination would have been to pull right back and harden my stance. Maybe I would have chosen a career based on reaction to my father, rather than the intrinsic suitability of it for my talents.

As it turned out, a couple of months of the golf pro career track was enough for me. Standing on the range day after day hitting golf balls is really hard work. It gives you a lot of time alone to think about the future. When you imagine yourself as a future golf pro, you see every bad shot as a threat to your career—and I hit plenty. But that wasn't the main thing. I could just tell that my heart and soul weren't in it.

So now what am I going to do? I thought. Back to square one. But not actually, as I had already eliminated a bunch of careers (see boys' dean, above). During my Taskforce year, I had become friends with the English teachers at my school, and they kept feeding me books. I had always loved to read, and I did a lot of reading that year. "Scott," they told me, "you should be an English major. It's about reading good books."

So I decided to return to Pacific Union College as an English major. Before, I'd never given a second thought to being an English major. I had associated it with grammar (which I hated). But once I got into a Victorian literature class, I discovered that I truly liked it, and I never looked back. However, let me return to the issue that sparked this chapter in the first place, that of having a calling, and see if I can justify this long digression on my personal history.

From my own experience, from reading the Bible, and from watching those around me, I believe the following:

*God has a place for us, maybe several places for us, and He will lead to the extent that we are leadable. At the same time, He created us as individuals and He prizes our uniqueness and our free will, and sometimes He just leaves decisions up to us.

*Regardless of what job we're doing, God has a consistent and clear desire for us to be looking out for the good of the community, serving others, and observing the basic principles of His kingdom.

*These days few jobs last forever. It's quite likely that many of you will change or modify careers during your lifetime, making it even more important that you see your life and general service to people as your calling, and your job as just one piece of that larger picture.

*It is quite likely (and a good thing, too) that we have talents in more than one area. And sometimes we enjoy things that we are not especially talented in. If we give our talents and interests to God, I truly believe that He will help us work out where to put our energies, and He will put us in a place where we can serve Him well.

If our career motivation is—as it seems to be for a number of the *Idol* contestants—to be recognized, remembered, applauded, I think we are looking through the wrong end of the telescope. Rather, I think we should concentrate on developing our gifts so that we can better serve the community and our Maker. If we can do that, we will have achieved something worthwhile.

Passage to consider: *Philippians 1:6.*

More TV

1. *Survivor*

CBS's hit show *Survivor*, which debuted in 2000, places 16 to 18 contestants in some remote location (Guatemala, the Australian outback, Pulau Tiga, etc.) and tests their survival skills. This includes living off the land, but more importantly, winning athletic and mental challenges and manipulating teammates and other competitors by means of alliances. In six years the show has had 12 "seasons"—anything profitable will get exploited to the max.

I find two aspects of the show engaging and enjoyable. The living off the land aspect is pretty interesting. Seeing the contestants get along without their usual food items, cigarettes, and alcohol (for the most part), and seeing them hunting for food, both plant and animal, building shelters, and repairing clothes appeals to those of us with an antimaterialistic side.

I also like the athletic contests. I've always enjoyed games, and the producers of this show are clever at coming up with ways for the tribes to combine brawn and brain. The contestants, though not current professional athletes, tend to be pretty athletic, but there's often an interesting intelligence aspect to the contests, so mere athleticism isn't enough.

The aspect of the show that gets me down and basically ruins any enjoyment from the other parts, however, is the way it is designed to undermine any relationships or natural human attachments. This happens because the losing tribe each week—and at a later stage in the show, the individual players—must vote one of their competitors off the island (or mainland, depending on the show's location).

There's a basic difference between this voting off and open competition in which a person tries his best and wins or loses based on his performance relative to the other competitors. In open competition you don't do anything dirty to try to win. Of course, pitchers throw the occasional spitball, and Mike Tyson may bite the occasional ear, but such actions are policed and penalized.

In *Survivor*, however, the very nature of the game encourages lying and backstabbing, and it is this ugly behavior itself that attracts the vulgar interest of much of the viewing audience. Of course, *Survivor* is only one of many reality TV shows that encourages low behavior in its participants to arouse viewer interest, and it's not the worst one, but the formation of alliances and double-crosses certainly runs directly contrary to any Christian ideals of community. To feed on this for entertainment purposes does to the moral nature something like what eating an eight-ounce brick of cheese at a meal does to the digestive system. (An unfortunate incident from yesterday's lunch brought this example to mind.)

Rather than casting people out of community, Christians are supposed to be drawing them in, looking for the outcasts and inviting them to the banquet Jesus has made ready for them (Luke 14). Christian philosophy is about team-building, inclusion.

2. The Sad Case of Richard Hatch

In the final show of the first season of *Survivor* (2000), a jury of competitors awarded Richard Hatch $1,000,000 as the most worthy survivor. As the closing credits rolled, Hatch spoke in a voice-over: "It's an amazing place to be. . . . I'm not exactly certain what I'm going to be doing with the million dollars. I hope to make the lives of my family and friends happier. I hope to remain who I am. I'm pretty certain I'll be able to do that. . . . I've won a car. That's just super. . . . [This is] an opportunity that I hope I don't waste."

Six years later, Hatch is beginning another survival ordeal. In January of 2006 a jury convicted him of two counts of tax evasion and one count of filing a false corporate return. In May he was sentenced to 51 months of prison, denied bail, and taken from the courtroom in handcuffs. In what seems to be an inexplicable combination of stupidity and cupidity, Hatch did not report the $1,000,000 prize (witnessed by an estimated 51 million persons) as part of his income on his tax return, nor the $10,000 that CBS paid him for a special appearance, nor the free car he received, nor $327,000 he earned as cohost of a Boston radio show, nor $28,000 he earned as rent from apartment buildings.

What takeaway points can we pick up here? We didn't need Hatch to teach us this, but human greed is pretty much limitless, and the more one acquires the more one wants—read the story of the rich fool in Luke 12. Why else would the exceedingly rich Kenneth Lay (Enron), Sam Waskal (ImClone), and Bernard Ebbers (WorldCom) do what they did?

But I'm intrigued that not only Hatch's competitors but the American public endorsed his questionable behavior on *Survivor* for its entertainment value, while we find the same behavior unacceptable in the real world. In other words, we might accept (or even applaud) behavior for entertainment that we wouldn't appreciate in a real-life neighbor, friend, or spouse. That seems like a dangerous road, something we should be very wary of.

We are told that "the heart is more deceitful than all else and is desperately sick" (Jeremiah 17:9), and reality TV, news shows, and even our own mirrors can bear that out abundantly. But we are also told "Blessed are the pure in heart, for they shall see God" (Matthew 5:8).

As a result of our fallen human condition, we are born with defective hearts. Yet God wants to repair them. He pours His love into our hearts (Romans 5:5), He sends His Spirit to minister to our hearts (Galatians 4:6), He will dwell in our hearts through faith (Ephesians 3:17), and He will comfort and strengthen our hearts (2 Thessalonians 2:17). God offers us, to paraphrase Hatch, a wonderful opportunity. Let's not waste it.

3. *The Biggest Loser*

When I first heard the name of the reality TV show *The Biggest Loser*, I thought *Oh brother, what new low have they hit in humiliating people on TV?* But upon investigating, I found that the show is a little different from what I expected. The premise is pretty simple: get a dozen or so grossly overweight people together and split them into two teams, each with a personal trainer.

Have them train over a period of 10 or 11 weeks (with one contestant being eliminated each week), and then have them continue training for three months independently. Then bring them back for a grand finale weigh-in, to see which contestant lost the biggest percentage of his or her starting weight. There is a similar opportunity for the nonfinalists to come back and demonstrate their weight loss.

Most reality shows encourage bad behavior, ranging from disgusting (*Fear Factor*) to greedy (*Deal or No Deal*), to self-promoting, ridiculous, campy, and immoral (many shows could qualify, but I'll mention *My Fair Brady*). *The Biggest Loser*, in contrast, encourages good behavior and positive lifestyle transformation.

All the contestants are significantly overweight to begin with. Their weight creates major health risks, social awkwardness, poor self-esteem, limited activities, and relationship difficulties. It pretty much dominates their lives. With the help of a dietician, physician, and personal trainer, *TBL* gives them a chance to change. The motivations, in addition to the desire to be healthier, include the public nature of their quest and a significant amount of money. But one of the best things about the show, in my opinion, is the number of times contestants comment that the money and winning are not as big a motivation or satisfaction as getting their bodies into shape.

But I wouldn't be writing about *TBL* if I didn't think there was a specific spiritual application—namely, an analogy between the show's premise and our spiritual situation here on earth. Fat is easy to see—it makes a great television visual, as does its absence. So let's imagine a little change in the laws of nature whereby character flaws and spiritual disorder, rather than excess food and lack of exercise, result in tremendous fat accumulation on our bodies. Of course those flaws are there—we just can't see them as easily as we can fat.

Jesus has volunteered to be our trainer. He will give us daily coaching to help us put healthy ingredients in our spiritual lives; He will give us workouts designed to sculpt and chisel our characters. In His imagination He can see the kind of people we can be if we—like Bob and Gillian—let Him work on us over time. However, like the trainers in *TBL*, He is limited. He can show us what we need to do, He can be there for us, but He can't actually do the workouts. Neither will He prevent us from making bad choices. So there's a definite part that we have to do, and it won't be easy.

But think of the rewards! In *TBL* the contestants enjoyed such rewards as being able to play basketball again, thrilling their spouses and family with their changes, being able to shop for clothes where most people shop, having energy and ability for many activities they'd given up in their obese state, and providing inspiration for many others. At the reunion show you could see the joy on their faces for the new persons they had become.

Of course, Satan will also be delighted to be our trainer, and will provide lots of specific exercises and tempting foods to bring about the spiritual and

45

character image that he has in mind for us. But he's not picky; he's also very willing for us to train on our own. The main thing, from his perspective, is that we don't work out with Jesus.

Thinking about the show, I got a new appreciation for a beautiful Bible passage, Philippians 3:18-21:

"For many walk, of whom I often told you, and now tell you even weeping, that they are enemies of the cross of Christ, whose end is destruction, whose god is their appetite, and whose glory is in their shame, who set their minds on earthly things.

"For our citizenship is in heaven, from which also we eagerly wait for a Savior, the Lord Jesus Christ; who will transform the body of our humble state into conformity with the body of His glory, by the exertion of the power that He has even to subject all things to Himself."

Satan has our destruction in mind, and a slow way and a fast way for us to get there. Jesus has a glorious destination for us, and He is doing everything possible to get us there. Someday we're going to have to step on those scales, so to speak, and the numbers will roll. Then it will be revealed whether we have become spiritually fit under our trainer or have ignored His advice. We will also see whether we have been an inspiration to those around us or a weight dragging them down. In *TBL* everyone can be a winner. The same is true in our real-life show.

4. *Deal or No Deal*

How's this for a game show idea? We have a contestant choose one of 26 briefcases to be his or her own, and the briefcase will contain a dollar designation somewhere between one cent and $1 million. In the course of several rounds, the contestant will eliminate the other briefcases, and for each round the host will offer the contestant a dollar amount to stop the game. For instance, after the first round, during which the contestant eliminates six briefcases, the host might offer $30,000 to stop. The contestant says either "Deal" and stops the game or "No deal" and continues. Almost all the players go pretty far into the game and a fevered pitch of excitement is reached as they must choose between, say, a deal for $76,000 or a briefcase, which may contain $300,000 or $100.

Most game shows make only modest intellectual demands, but the brain bar is set particularly low for *Deal or No Deal*. There is no trivia to answer, no prices to calculate, only the naked opposition of greed and prudence. Oh, and—sexism is not dead!—a pretty female model holds up each briefcase.

In order to foment the emotional factor, expressive contestants are chosen, and each of them selects an entourage of friends and relatives who sit or stand in a little "on deck" circle to the side, offering encouragement and advice. It gets kind of crazy toward the end of the game when the audience is yelling "No deal," the husband is yelling "Deal," and the best friend is freaking out with her hands pressed to her cheeks.

The host, Howie Mandel, has an interesting rationale for the show's popularity: "I think the whole goal of humanity is to get and acquire for doing as little as possible. And a game show is the perfect environment for doing that." How do you, as a human being, as a Christian, feel about that characterization? If that is true for us, if we are a victim of game show mentality, then may Heaven help us change!

The consequences of *Deal or No Deal* can seem enormous—the chance to get out of debt, build a new house, go on a cruise, buy the new Lexus or whatever toy that reality has cruelly prevented poor Johnny from getting. But in one sense, even before the first stage light comes on, all the people on the show are losers, audience included, because they are all there to celebrate a warped sense of the value of money. Our heavenly Father has promised us that He will take care of our needs (Matthew 6:25-34); in fact, He will abundantly supply more than we could think or ask for (Ephesians 3:20). Not that this will generally be material goods, which is not the point anyway. As Jesus says in Luke 12:15, "Beware, and be on your guard against every form of greed; for not even when one has an abundance does his life consist of his possessions."

It's not just Howie Mandel, we should remember, who is in the deal-making business. God too makes us an offer. It's not a guessing game; there's no designer-gowned model holding up briefcases. But the terms are just as clear: forgiveness of sins (Ephesians 1:7); meaning and purpose in life; the Holy Spirit to guide us to the truth (John 16:13); the fruits of the Spirit (Galatians 5:22, 23); status as sons and daughters of God (2 Corinthians 6:18).

Deal or no deal?

PART 2: Movies

Movies

1. *The Truman Show*

"We accept the reality of the world we're presented with," says Christof, the tyrannical director of the show within *The Truman Show* (1998).

You may recall the premise of this movie, that the main character, Truman (Jim Carrey), is a real person who unknowingly has lived on a gigantic movie set from birth. His wife, his best friend since childhood, his neighbors, his colleagues at work, people he passes on the street—all are cast members, creating a staged world around Truman. The film provides a fascinating examination of the nature of reality and has a number of points of interest from a Christian perspective.

First of all, it's a study of the relationship of a created being and his creator. Since Truman's birth, the godlike Christof has followed and shaped Truman's life. He literally makes the sun rise every morning by cueing the appropriate lighting effects. He controls the weather, the people Truman meets, Truman's job, and many other aspects of his life. We assume that he even chose Truman's (actor) wife. He "loves" Truman, in a manner that we will examine further along.

As the story gets rolling, the audience (and later Truman) begins noticing little departures from ordinary reality. Seahaven, the town where Truman lives, looks too perfect, as if Disney World employees had removed every speck of litter and lawn clippings. Although we're not sure what it is at the time, a stage light from the sky crashes on the street. And the people Truman meets seem to act just a little strange.

Finally one day as Truman is driving to work he accidentally hears the transmission from the show's control center identifying his car's progress and alerting the next group of extras to be ready for their cues. Truman doesn't hear quite enough to be sure of what he has happened upon, but putting different clues together, he suddenly begins to perceive that the "reality" around him may have a very different character from that which he has always believed.

Christians should really be able to identify with this point, and should ponder it. As I'm sitting here typing, through the window I see the breeze blowing through the leaves of the trees and the shadow of the building creeping along the grass as the sun declines in the west. These are the obvious realities I can see.

But I also believe in a number of things I can't see and, like Truman, I don't fully understand. My guardian angel is somewhere around, doing what, from my perspective, must be a pretty boring job. God is out there, and also in here, in my head, if He cares to be. Jesus lived on earth a couple thousand years ago, died, and was resurrected. Right there you have enough beliefs to put me out of the rationalist/materialist camp.

Not only do I believe these things, but I act on them every day. I pray for others; I ask for the Holy Spirit to illumine my mind as I study the Bible, as I talk with a student, as I write this book. I believe in certain moral absolutes, such as the Ten Commandments. I adopt and stand by certain values because of my Bible study, not just because they seem useful. In other words, this second level of reality, if you will, has a distinct and vital impact on the way I act in the first level of reality. I am, as the title of a book by Roger Dudley and Edwin Hernandez phrases it, a "citizen of two worlds."

In the beginning Truman thinks that he is a citizen of one world, that what he sees is all there is, but little by little he begins to see the cracks in his world that hint at a greater reality beyond: the falling skylight, that fact that he is always cut off when he tries to get beyond the island, the radio transmission, his wife's goofy presentation of material goods as if they were commercials—which they are.

Truman's situation of dawning consciousness is comparable to that faced by materialists—people who believe that the surface reality of this world is all there is. There are hints of another, greater reality: in the faith and purpose of a Mother Teresa (she has to be called in as an example in every contemporary religious book, and now she's made it into this one), the manifestations of altruistic love that most people see somewhere around them, the inadequacy of material goods to satisfy human nature, conscience . . . there are a lot of different things that can get us thinking about a bigger reality.

Truman is a tiger. Contradicting Christof's belief, "We accept the reality of the world we're presented with," once he realizes that there might be another reality beyond all he knows, Truman refuses to accept the reality he's lived in since birth. He is even willing to confront his fear of water and the tremendous storm and physical danger that Christof wreaks on him in an attempt to save *The Truman Show.*

This brings us back to the relationship of creator and created. Christof, in the story's climax, tries to talk Truman out of leaving his world. He points out the sense of security that that world brings. He calls on Truman's sense of loyalty, appreciation, or even love for himself, Christof.

Truman will have none of it. Opening the door to the real world, he dismisses Christof with the tagline he's used so often to greet his neighbors: "Good afternoon, good evening, and good night." The movie ends with Truman stepping out the door into an unknown world, hoping, perhaps, to find Sylvia, the one real woman he'd fallen in love with—the woman, not the actor, who'd been abruptly fired from the show when producers realized his feelings.

Christof, unlike God, is a manipulator, someone who is only interested in Truman in so far as he can create glory and high ratings for Christof. He is willing to put Truman's life at stake for defying him. Although he acts tenderly toward Truman, we are able to see that his tenderness is only a sort of disguised self-love for his own creation, as long as it acts within the boundaries he has established for it.

Fortunately, "Christ-on," as we might say, is identified first and foremost for His character of love, self-sacrificing love, for His creation. In the reality show He created, He was willing to pay any price to secure the good of His creatures and to preserve their freedom. Furthermore, He has given them lots of hints about the behind-the-scenes reality of their world, and a direct and open line to Him.

Over the years Truman constructed a composite woman in Sylvia's image from dozens of magazine photos of different women. Sylvia is Truman's answer for what is beyond his painted world. She stands for an alternate reality, if only he can get to her. For the Christian, something much better is waiting for us on the other side of this earthly reality—a God whose composite image we should be working hard to assemble each day from the resources available to us. Sylvia wears a button that says "How's it going to end?" That's the question each of us needs to explore.

2. *Shrek*

Shrek (2001) was a great box office success and a highly entertaining film, with Eddie Murphy's comedic donkey, a number of clever cameos by fairy-tale characters, and some creative twists on traditional fairy-tale plotting. One of those twists is of particular interest from a Christian perspective. It consists of reexamining the relationship of physical beauty and size (our outer self) to moral nature (our inner self).

You may recall that, as in a traditional fairy tale, *Shrek* has a beautiful princess locked in the top of a remote castle, guarded by a fire-breathing dragon. The aspirants to be the princess's rescuer and potential mate, however, are not the usual assortment of knights.

Whereas movies and magazines perpetually inundate us with images of conventional beauty—for women, that would currently consist of being considerably taller and slimmer than average, with perfect teeth, highlighted hair, a perpetual pout, and so on—*Shrek* succeeds by going against type. The title character is green, oversized, heavy on top, and on the crude side, with ears that look like the bells of trumpets. Not to mention gaps in his teeth. But Shrek is an ogre, and we expect an ogre to be ugly.

Things get more interesting with Lord Farquaad, Shrek's rival. He has a Kirk Douglas hero's jaw, striking black hair, and perfect teeth—and a pushy, egocentric personality. He would be a conventional villain, except for one thing—he's about the height of a fire hydrant. Some people might see this as an attempt to make fun of short people, and maybe there's a little of that in it. His (lack of) height is a subject of some jest.

But I think there's a more interesting way of viewing his and Shrek's relative size. The oversized Shrek and undersized Lord are expanded to the size of their moral nature. Wouldn't it be interesting, and cause for considerable adjustment in our perceptions, if everyone grew or shrank according to the level of his or her moral nature? As one who is six feet four inches and at least dimly aware of a number of character deficiencies, I would have special cause for concern. But the laws of nature do not correlate the size of our inner and outer natures.

There are, however, some standards that usually apply to beauty and happy endings. The hero and heroine must be beautiful. Well, there can be some flexibility with the hero, but at least the heroine must be beautiful. *Shrek* also turns this idea on its end by having Princess Fiona turn into an ogre each night and, at the end of the movie, having Shrek tell her that she is beautiful as such and that he loves her just that way.

Following *Shrek*, we have not had a rash of movies with "ugly" heroes and heroines; there's a part of us that likes to continually fantasize about being prettier than we are. But I think that *Shrek* was partly popular because the average viewer is—believe it or not—of average height and looks. The media typically promote an image of physical beauty and an attention to physical beauty that makes us average people feel pretty inadequate. *Shrek* makes an interesting and convincing statement in a contrary direction, and I think that's a good thing.

By the way, we have physical descriptions of a few people in the Bible. We know that Goliath was exceptionally tall (1 Samuel 17) and Zaccheus was short (Luke 19), Bathsheba was very beautiful (2 Samuel 11) and Eglon was very fat (Judges 3). However, we are given no physical description of Jesus, which is perhaps surprising, considering that there is much more written about Him than about any of the characters just mentioned. If God, say, had some reasons to exclude a description of Jesus' physical characteristics, what might some of those reasons be?

Passages to consider: *1 Samuel 16:7; Proverbs 31:30.*

3. *Titanic*

The other day I was perusing a Web site that listed the 100 biggest American box office films of all time. *How curious*, I thought, *that the top money-making film, Titanic, was, in my opinion, one of the worst films I ever saw.*

Let me back up a little. In 1997, when the film came out, I was teaching a class in film analysis, and several of my students strongly encouraged me to go see *Titanic*. So even though I go to a theater only about as often as we change presidents, I did go off to see *Titanic*—and in one way I thought it was magnificent.

Pretty much everything to do with the size and beauty of the ship, and the way it was photographed, was awesome. There were a number of breathtaking flyovers, long shots of the ship against the horizon, beautiful dissolves from the wreck of the ship to the ship at the height of its glory, and shots of the title characters at the prow of the ship, breeze blowing back their hair, basking in the thrill of riding one of man's greatest creations across the vastness of the ocean.

What I had trouble swallowing was the invented story of Jack and Rose within the larger historical drama. Leonardo DiCaprio has never interested me, but it's more than that. I think it was the monstrous bag of unlikely plot twists and coincidences that I was asked to hoist on my back and carry through the story. Let me mention just the first 25 that come to mind.

1. Rose climbs over the rear of the ship and stands on the far side of the railing undetected. On a ship with more than 2,000 passengers and crew?

2. Jack arrives in the nick of time and talks her out of committing suicide, and no other passengers intrude.

3. However, ship personnel do arrive at the precise moment when Jack and Rose fall into a compromising position.

4. Molly Brown happens to be packing a tuxedo from her absent son.

5. She loans it to Jack, a person she hardly knows.

6. It fits him perfectly.

7. Jack pulls off a creditable performance at dinner with the rich folks.

8. Jack teaches Rose to spit.

9. Cal and his servant (Lovejoy) are almost insanely malevolent and malicious toward Jack.

10. Rose initiates posing in the nude for Jack.

11. Jack draws her with complete artistic restraint.

12. They have just enough time to do all this, write a note, return the diamond to the safe, and leave the room a moment before Lovejoy arrives.

13. They consummate their brief acquaintance (at Rose's insistence) in a conveniently located luxury car in a well-lighted storage room, and again, finish just in time to dress and depart as ship's personnel arrive at the room to search for them.

14. Lovejoy plants a diamond in streetwise Jack's pocket just as he walks into the room to help Rose warn her mother about impending disaster.

15. Rose is able to descend three flights of stairs, wade through waist-high water, and find Jack, handcuffed to a pipe in the ship's brig.

16. Rose leaves Jack, finds an ax, returns, and after two wild practice strokes precisely severs Jack's handcuffs just before the rising water would

have overcome him.

17. Jack and Rose get through several locked doors and grates just in time to escape watery disasters.

18. Cal fires eight shots from a revolver at Jack and Rose, each time coming close but missing.

19. As Rose is being lowered in a lifeboat, she has a change of heart and is able to leap off on a lower deck and run into Jack's arms once again.

20. Rose, who is almost dead from cold, is able to climb off her floating "raft" and swim to a dead man who has a whistle, and successfully whistle to a rescue boat.

21. Rose wears Cal's overcoat through all these latter stages.

22. Rose keeps Cal's incredibly valuable diamond for 80 some years, never telling anyone about it, and then drops it into the ocean for a dramatic end to the movie.

23. Rose never tells "Grandfather," the man to whom she was married for many years, about Jack, because "a woman's heart is a deep ocean of secrets."

24. However, Rose does narrate this most intimate tale to her granddaughter and about 20 strangers.

25. Rose has a cockeyed dream that—amidst the actual tragedy of the historical narrative—allows the film to have the sappiest of Hollywood endings, as she is reunited with Jack on the grand staircase landing in front of all the cheering passengers and crew of *Titanic*.

I have been thinking about why this grab bag of improbability especially bothers me in *Titanic*. After all, it might not bother me so much—indeed, it might prove part of the humor—in, say, a Bob Hope "Road" movie. Well, perhaps that's it. Maybe in a comedy or an action adventure movie we are willing to allow a little more in the way of improbability, but the serious historical nature of the subject matter of the sinking of the *Titanic*, and the tragedy suffered by so many people with that event, makes it almost an insult to the actuality of the real event to have such a hokey story inserted into it. It's the juxtaposition of a fantastical bit of hogwash within a real tragedy that I find disgusting.

Just two more points, and I will let *Titanic* rest at the bottom. The movie paints a seriously distorted picture of what love is by presenting a choice between two bad options as if it were a choice between a bad and a good option. Cal (Rose's spoiled, rich fiancé), is shown to be selfish, malicious, a cheater, physically abusive, an out and out terrible guy. He shows this so dramatically and consistently throughout the movie that it's very hard to believe that Rose would ever have engaged herself to him. But we're supposed to believe that she did because of pressure from her mother to marry Cal for his money.

On the other hand we have Jack Dawson, who talks Rose out of committing suicide, helps her escape her conventional self to become her "true" self (as exhibited in teaching her how to spit), is a good artist, and willingly draws her in the nude, makes love to her, then tragically dies. Jack and Rose's love affair is held up as a model to viewers, and I think that's a real problem.

It implies that the ideal love is much more passionate than thoughtful, and consists mainly in throwing away the boundaries of using your head, reason, and patience in favor of passion, spontaneity, and doing what feels right in the moment. The only way that can look good in the film is by contrast to the horrific prospect of marriage to Cal. It's a false proposition.

By the way, in addition to her torrid 48 hours with Jack, Rose was married, presumably for many years, to a man referred to as "Grandfather." Presumably they were happily married. However, that relationship isn't filmable or tragic/romantic in the same way, and gets only a sentence of mention in the film. Grandfather, indeed, was never even informed of Rose's relationship with Jack (see number 23 above). The relationship with Jack is grossly overvalued, within the context of the film, compared to the relationship with Grandfather.

A second false proposition comes in a statement from the elderly Rose near the end of the film. She says, to the crew of the *Titanic* recovery ship, to whom she tells her personal story of the disaster, "Jack saved me in every way that a person can be saved." This statement seems to have two basic applications. First, that Jack saved her life in the physical sense by helping her through the last minutes before *Titanic* sunk, getting her onto some floating debris, and giving her a pep talk about going on. Second, Jack saved her "spiritually" by getting her to break away from her relationship to Cal and the false world of ideals that included. We see, as evidence of this, that she is an accomplished potter in her old age, a craftsperson, an artist.

Let us not, as Christians, permit such a statement to pass unchallenged. I am all for escaping from materialism and developing personal creativity, but do I consider that the highest form of salvation? Absolutely not. As Christians we have a much higher conception of "salvation" than that, and if we fall into believing the *Titanic* myths about love and salvation, then, fellow passengers, we are really sunk.

Passages to consider: *Acts 4:12; Romans 1:16; 1 Thessalonians 5:9; 1 Timothy 4:16; Hebrews 2:3.*

4. *Crash*

I just finished watching *Crash*. Wow. What an amazing movie. It is an "R" movie for some of the usual reasons, but for mature viewers it has some definite value, including many insights about living in a multicultural environment. The story takes place in contemporary Los Angeles, and features characters from various communities within the Asian, Black, White, Middle Eastern, and Latino worlds.

At the beginning of the film, one of the characters offers this philosophy about living in L.A.: "In any real city, you walk, you know? You brush past people, people bump into you. In L.A., nobody touches you. We're always behind this metal and glass. I think we miss that touch so much that we crash into each other just so we can feel something." As a native of Southern California, I don't wish to deny L.A.'s uniqueness, but I think the film is more about the things humans from all parts of the country share—though L.A., of course, is an excellent location to show high intensity cross-cultural exchanges.

The film does an excellent job of showing stereotypes in action, while fighting the action of stereotyping. For example, two young Black men have a lively discussion about stereotyping done by Whites against Blacks and by Black women against Black men. Then you suddenly see them whip guns out of their jackets—they're carjackers, fitting neatly into a young Black urban male stereotype. But as we follow these characters through the film, we find out that you can never pigeonhole someone, and each character reveals surprising new sides.

The same is true for a bad White cop (played by Matt Dillon), who uses his police authority to humiliate a Black couple. Later in the film, he is shown to be a caring man for his aged and ailing father, and given a second chance, he rescues from a car accident one of the Black people he humiliated earlier in the film.

One of the most interesting things about *Crash* is the way it shows how pretty much everyone has some racism in them. Characters may seem above or beyond that, but when they get in a tight spot, the racism comes out. Contrarily, and this is carefully and credibly illustrated, racist characters can also rise above their racism and do noble and even heroic things across racial lines, and there is a special beauty and uplifting of spirit when this happens.

When one of the main characters, who happens to be a detective, finds out that his younger brother has been shot and left dead at the side of the road, he promises his mother that he will find the person who did this. In a telling moment, the mother says, "I already know who killed him. You did. I told you to find your brother, but you were too busy for us." The mother is not literally correct, in that her older son had nothing to do with the immediate cause of the brother's death. But her comment points out a larger truth about human interdependency and responsibility.

Cain's comment, "Am I my brother's keeper?" (Genesis 4:9), naturally comes to mind. Cain chose a particularly bad moment for saying this, inasmuch as he had just killed his brother. Yes, he was clearly responsible for the absence of Abel. But we are all our brothers' and sisters' keepers in a much larger sense. Jesus tried to get this point across in a number of settings, including the parable of the good Samaritan (Luke 10), the parable of the rich man and Lazarus (Luke 16), and in His encounter with the Samaritan woman (John 4).

But probably my favorite verse on this topic is Galatians 3:28: "There is neither Jew nor Greek, there is neither slave nor free man, there is neither male nor female; for you are all one in Christ Jesus." If I am ever tempted to think in a racist manner—and the devil will attack us on any point in which he thinks he can gain a victory—I ask God to bring this verse to mind. The sentence has four parts. The first implicitly says that for the Christian there are no racial boundaries; the second states that there are no class boundaries; the third asserts that there are no gender boundaries; the fourth explains how the first three can be possible: "you are all one in Christ Jesus." In Christ Jesus.

We can't be "one" just by pulling up our bootstraps and agreeing that racism is ugly. We need outside help. A truth that helps me think about carrying out Galatians 3:28 is found in 1John 4:7-21, namely that God is love, that God will give us His love, and that perfect love casts out fear.

Crash shows a metropolitan area teetering on the brink of disaster. People are full of fear, mistrustful, and suspicious. They're stereotyping others, changing locks on their doors, yelling at each other, buying handguns—and some of it is justified. But as the film draws to its close, it also shows how love can animate people to beautiful actions, how it is the contrary power to all the bad things we have seen throughout the movie.

The movie doesn't delve into where love—the counterpower to all this fear and suspicion—comes from. It just shows it naturally welling up. And it sometimes appears that way: we just love because we love, or hate because we hate. However, that point of view makes us seem more at the mercy of circumstances than we really are. It definitely makes more sense to me that, as the Bible informs us, there is an outside source for love. It doesn't come from Hallmark, the FTD florist, or chocolate kisses. It doesn't just bubble up automatically, "for love is from God; and everyone who loves is born of God and knows God" (1 John 4:7).

One of the key lines of the film comes from Matt Dillon's character, the (sometimes) bad cop: "You think you know who you are. You have no idea." This is a warning to a young, idealistic cop, who later, caught in a web of unfortunate circumstances, kills a Black hitchhiker in what he thinks is self-defense. Dillon's character is correct in implying that human beings, on their own, cannot be sure of their future moral or immoral actions. But human beings can be sure of where to turn for moral guidance and assistance. It is (fallen) human nature to crash, but it is God's delight to restore broken people of all kinds to valuable roles in the human community.

Postscript: When I first watched the film, I didn't recognize the depth of its portrayal of humanity's spiritual aspect. After watching about half of it again, and listening to the director's commentary track, I would point out three noteworthy attempts in this direction.

The most obvious is the musical score. Much of the background music is the sort of ethereal chorus or lone voice that suggests a spiritual perspective on our planet's condition, a distancing, almost as if we are viewing human tragedy from outside, hearing, as Matthew Arnold puts it, "the eternal note of sadness." OK, getting pretty far out on the subjective pole, I hear the voice lamenting the miserable way in which humans treat each other, and doing so from the perspective of a higher, loftier conscience.

A second spiritual angle in the film is created through the motif of sprinkling crosses through the film, literal crosses, in some cases, but more often symbolic ones, such as the telephone pole with crossbeam behind the health insurance mediator's window, or the painted street lines in the final helicopter shot. The crosses are just a subtle reminder of the larger spiritual context in which humans operate. So subtle that, I confess, I missed it the first time through the film. Oops.

Finally, there's the idea of snow coming to Los Angeles at the end of the film, a sort of miracle in itself. It's talked about at a few points through the film, and then it descends in the last few minutes as some of the characters connect at a deeper level with their true selves, connect with their significant others, restore relationships. The snow appears almost like a manifestation of grace, coming out of the sky and making the ugly old earth have a special beauty.

Which brings up one last point. A good film will stand up to repeated viewings—offering new insights and new food for thought. This is also true—even more true—of God's Word.

5. *The Conscientious Objector*

Desmond T. Doss has a remarkable story. It has been told twice in book form, first as *The Unlikeliest Hero*, by Booton Herndon (Pacific Press, 1967), the book I read when I was a kid, and more recently as *Desmond Doss in God's Care*, by Frances Doss (The College Press, 1998). In 2004, director/producer Terry Benedict released a feature-length documentary on Doss's story, *The Conscientious Objector*.

Although Benedict had long wanted to make a Doss film, when he got the opportunity the task was daunting, and not just because money is almost always a challenge in moviemaking. There were many ways the story could be told, many pieces to the story. How would Benedict find and assemble the pieces and create a compelling composite?

The final product uses old photographs, letters, newspaper clippings and newsreel footage, panels from a 1940s comic book version of Doss's story, interviews with veterans who served with Doss, visits to places important to the story, landscape shots, interviews with Doss's brother and sister, and interviews with Doss himself.

Perhaps the most important document is the illustrated Ten Commandments that hung on the wall of the Doss home when Desmond was growing up. This is a story about a man who was anchored in the highest ideals from a young age, and the commandments were his anchor. Receiving special attention in the film are the fourth and sixth commandments, about observing the Sabbath and about not killing. In this story we see how Doss was repeatedly put to the test with regard to both commandments, and his integrity under extreme pressure is very moving.

In our day we often confuse hero with celebrity, and it's good to be reminded of the difference. Doss is a not a hero for being able to slam-dunk, for having a handsome jawline or marrying Jennifer Lopez, but rather for his moral stature. This is amply illustrated by numerous incidents recounted in the film that culminate in the astounding feat, on Okinawa in 1945, of lowering approximately 75 men over Hacksaw Ridge during 12 hours of intense combat. But a person doesn't achieve that kind of heroic feat in a vacuum, without a specific background leading up to it.

A quote from Emerson opens the film: "Whoso would be a man must be a nonconformist." H'mmm. That's quite a bit to think about. Well, this film is about how 99 people out of 100 were going one direction, and Doss went the other way. First of all, Doss had no compulsion to join the Army. As a worker in a shipbuilding facility, he was offered a deferment. He would have had no stigma attached to him for working the war in a safe factory, not to mention that when Pearl Harbor was bombed, he had just recently married. Nevertheless, Doss insisted on enlisting and putting himself in harm's way for the good of his country.

His country was far from immediately grateful. In basic training Doss suffered tremendous pressure to alter his conscientious objector status and bear arms, including threats of court-martial from superior officers and constant hounding from the other soldiers. According to a fellow soldier, Doss "was 100 percent in his religious beliefs, and he just disregarded what [these others] said." That Doss could remain supportive of his country and willing to put his life on the line time and again for "his men" after the way he was treated illustrates extraordinary selflessness.

The sections of the film I appreciated most were the ample yet well-selected interviews with veterans, soldiers who served with Doss. You see the deeply lined faces (often juxtaposed with their handsome young poses in uniform more than a half century earlier), the labored steps, the age spots, and you listen to the voices calling up vivid memories, tinctured with the perspective of old age. There are some wonderful extreme close-ups of mouths, fingers, lips, as the story comes out.

You see how these articulate old men are really attached to Doss, to the ideals he stood for. You see how they could have changed from teasing him and belittling him to holding him up with respect and awe at what he accomplished when the machine-gun bullets were thick overhead and the strongest men doubted.

And finally you see Desmond, with his "reedy" voice, as one reviewer put it, his slow movements, his speech impediment (associated with his deafness), his plain way of speaking, his simplicity, his humility, and you try to comprehend what he did and how he did it all those years ago. Doss is quick to give the glory to God. Of his time on the ridge he says "I was praying the whole time. I was just praying 'Lord, please help me get one more.'

"From a human standpoint," says Doss, "I shouldn't be here to tell the story. All the glory should go to God. No telling how many times the Lord has spared my life" (the Richmond *Times-Dispatch*, 1998).

I appreciate Doss's heroism because it shows what a person committed to serving God can accomplish, and his example makes me want to be that kind of person too. Doss died in March 2006, but we have the opportunity to carry on his legacy by connecting to the source of Doss's power. Near the end of the film Benedict say that Doss's "whole being was so profound that it changed the world around him." If we are faithful to God, we too will change the world—for good.

Passage to consider: *Matthew 5:13-16.*

6. *Jonah,* a VeggieTales Movie

The ancient Roman Horace (65 to 8 B.C.), in his *Art of Poetry*, gave us a guideline that has informed much criticism of the arts since his time. Horace identified twin objectives for poetry (by extension, these apply to other arts) of instructing and delighting.

Instruction could include reading a John Grisham novel to learn about the legal system, a biography of Lord Nelson to learn of British naval history during Napoleonic times, *Sophie's World* to learn about philosophy, *Christ's Object Lessons* to learn about interpreting the parables, the ESPN Web page to find out how Michelle Wie is playing in the latest golf tournament—not very well, likely. We all read because we want to increase our knowledge.

We also read for pleasure, to be delighted. In one sense this is a false distinction, because increasing our knowledge is itself a very important cause of pleasure. But it makes sense to use this as a separate category, since it allows us to identify qualities such as beauty, humor, perfection of form, felicity of expression, as sources of great pleasure in interacting with a work and not related to learning per se.

In great works of art, you usually get both instruction and delight, though in differing ratios. For instance, Psalm 33 is both beautifully written and has a wonderful and important message, and I think it is unlikely that people would care so much about the message if it were not put in such a memorable package.

I say all this as background to my discussion of VeggieTales because I have ambivalent feelings about the series. I like the way the original story of Jonah is told in the Bible. Now that I write that sentence I smile, because the story of Jonah in the Bible is probably not the first time the story was told. I would imagine that Jonah himself told the earlier parts of the story many times in Nineveh, and that the written story included in the Old Testament followed many oral tellings.

I was going to say, however, that I like the clean, simple approach of the biblical version, and I don't know that I want dancing vegetables interfering with my appreciation of the "original" narrative. I ask myself questions such as, "Does all this hooting and hollering, the jokes and the Broadway routines, detract from or add to the message?" I'll come back to this.

Meanwhile, from an entertainment perspective, there are a lot of clever things in *Jonah*, the movie. The integration of the interpolated tale of Jonah within a modern family adventure is well-done, the writing is clever, the integration of anachronistic artifacts (such as a television set and modern advertising) within the biblical context is humorous and updates the story, and even the Broadway style production number in the belly of the whale works at some level. One of the most clever angles of the story is the invention of Khalil, the little caterpillar-worm traveling buddy of Jonah. He has an entertaining accent, an irrepressible, loquacious personality, and, actually, a place in the original text as the worm in Jonah 4:7. The script is smart and self-aware without getting too full of itself. In short, I'd rate the entertainment value of the film pretty high.

And in terms of getting across the core message of Jonah, I'd say that it's also pretty good. Wedged in between all the entertainment is a clear message about how God treats us with compassion and mercy, how He gives us second chances, how great that is, and how we should treat others likewise (note the passage to consider). There's even an interesting twist on the "incomplete" ending of "Jonah"—the narrative doesn't tell us what Jonah did next after complaining to God about His sparing Nineveh. So the character who is telling the story of Jonah to some children says, "The question, my friend, is not 'What did Jonah learn?' The question is 'What did you learn?'"

So yes, I think that *VeggieTales* does a good job of identifying the core message of this story (and others in its series of productions) and packaging it in an entertaining and hip modern production. Is it for everyone? No, and I don't consider myself a big *VeggieTales* fan. But I do think that they're doing a great job at creating programming that has good values, has a biblical basis, and will appeal to a secular market. And that's something to get excited about.

If you're interested in a well-done analytic study of *VeggieTales* that further discusses the question of how entertaining a Christian ministry should be, try this book: *There's Never Been a Show Like Veggie Tales: Sacred Messages in a Secular Market*, by Hillary Warren (AltaMira Press, 2005).

Passage to consider: *Jonah 4:6-11.*

7. Superheroes

When I was a kid, I used to watch Spider-Man cartoons once in a while (along with *Underdog* and *Ultraman*). In this generation, superheroes seem pretty popular once again, what with a new Superman movie in 2006, a new Spider-Man movie in 2007, and even an Underdog movie scheduled for 2007. Not to mention the X-Men movies, the Batman movies, *The Incredibles, My Super Ex-Girlfriend*, and on down the caped marvels chain.

What is it with superheroes that makes them so popular? Is it mainly a guy thing? Is there anything for a Christian to learn from thinking, at least briefly, about the superhero phenomenon? How is Jesus like and unlike a superhero? This past week I watched the original *Superman* movie (1978), along with *Spider-Man* (2002), and tried to come up with some answers to—or at least some thoughts about—these pressing questions.

Let's start with the obvious. It's fun (at least for the first 10 minutes) to watch idealized human beings in designer unitards smacking evil upside the head. Superheroes are physically idealized, Greek statues in motion, and since most of us can't get this satisfaction from looking in the mirror, we take pleasure in looking at physically idealized human beings in movies, magazines, and sporting events. Modern Western society is very visually oriented, and superheroes work well within that context.

Then there's that costume. At first it seems superficial, just something to stock discount store shelves leading up to Halloween, but there's a couple more points worth observing. Superman and Spider-Man both have conventional identities as well as superhero identities. In their conventional identities, they have challenges at work, conflicts with the boss, and relationship challenges, and there's nothing especially attractive about them. In other words, they're like us.

But underneath the conventional identity is this alter ego, the superhero, who is all the things the conventional person is not. I can identify with that. I mean, it's fun to imagine myself with a 40-inch vertical leap, toothpaste-ad teeth, George Clooney's hair, and . . . this could be a long list. The point is, we all have an image of what we could be—if only. The costume marks the transition from one identity to the other.

In this context, Spider-Man's mask is especially potent. As long as he's masked, his identity is hidden—anonymous. In fact, it could be you or me on the end of that web, swinging from building to building or having the female hero roll up the mask just enough for a kiss. The mask aids viewers with the dubious pleasure of projection, vicariously playing the superhero role.

Then there's the angle that these guys are doing something important, something that matters. Compare saving the world, or even stopping three or four felonious assaults, to my job this evening of mowing the lawn. Superheroes live in a world of excitement, where their actions matter tremendously to those around them. Identifying with them can give us a feeling of vicarious significance, even as it makes our own lives seem even more mundane by comparison.

I think all this projection must be a particularly human thing. Maybe the dachshunds down the street dream of being Great Danes, but I doubt it. It's humans who have the big imaginations about what they could be, as well as a sense of falling short. But what about Jesus as a superhero?

Well, there are some similarities. Like to Superman, He came from somewhere else. He has special powers. He is vital to the struggle of good against evil on Planet Earth. He has a sort of dual identity as human and God. But who is copying whom? If any imitating is taking place, it's coming from the superhero side.

The original *Superman* movie begins on the planet Krypton, where the people walk around in blinding white suits. Jor-El, Superman's father (Marlon Brando), is passing judgment on three traitors who have, in the great controversy style, rebelled against the government of Krypton. The leader of the rebels pleads with Jor-El to join him and promises that Jor-El will be second in command in the new order. When Jor-El refuses, the devil counterpart asserts to Jor-El that someday "you will bow before me." Years later, Superman has a "visitation" from his dead father, who lays out his son's purpose in life in Christlike terms: Earth "can be a great people . . . they lack only the light to show the way. For this reason, I have sent them you, my only son." The biblical phrasing and imagery are unmistakable. So in certain clear ways Superman, though ironically created by Jewish writers, has clear parallels with Christ.

And Superman, like Christ, has a clear archenemy (Lex Luthor) who wants to take over the earth at great cost to its inhabitants. It's up to Superman to put his life on the line for the benefit of his adopted people. At this point the differences become more instructive than the similarities.

Jesus, unlike the superheroes, has no designer costume. He wore the clothes of the people of His day, except for when He was transfigured. Clothes did not emphasize the body in Jesus' time and place, and it seems strikingly incongruous to imagine Him as particularly buff and proud of it. Unlike the superheroes, Jesus didn't access His special powers whenever He got in a jam. And unlike them, He didn't avail himself of any special martial arts abilities or special weapons. In fact, He didn't get into any physical combats with His archenemy, the sine qua non of the superhero movie.

The point about the martial arts showdown scene merits further discussion. Why would it seem so ridiculous for Jesus, say, in Pilate's courtroom, to suddenly strip off His robes and fly around the room laying out Roman soldiers with a series of scissor kicks, punches, feints, and flips? For someone purely human, of course, this wouldn't be an option because of human physical limitations. But Jesus could have called on His divine powers to slap or zap without breaking a sweat. Why is Jesus so different from the superheroes on this crucial point? For one thing, the superheroes operate in an intensely visual medium. In film, "Will it look good?" is a constant criterion. And in our overstimulated culture, looking good generally means visually exciting, active, in motion. The climactic fight between the superhero and his archenemy perfectly fits this requirement.

Beyond this, however, is the question of means of persuasion. How does

good vanquish evil? In the superhero movie, it's almost always a physical contest. Whoever is strongest, quickest, or has the best weapons subdues the
opponent. And there's a pattern that's so predictable that it's boring. The archenemy at first has some new gadget or plot that temporarily gains him (99
percent of the time it's a him) the upper hand, but in the final battle, after taking some severe knocks and looking like his goose is cooked, our superhero
rises one last time and decks the prematurely gloating archenemy for good.
Or until the next sequel.

In Jesus' narrative, however, encounters with the archenemy are limited.
There are those unforgettable encounters in which the devil tempts Jesus
(Matthew 4), but notice that the encounters are entirely verbal—well, maybe
there were some interesting facial expressions, too. And, of course, we assume that the devil is there in the background during Jesus' trial and crucifix-
ion, as well as throughout His ministry.

Jesus' primary encounters throughout His recorded biography in the
gospels, however, are with people, not the archenemy. He is partly on earth
to "fight" the devil, yes, but the bulk of His time is spent tending to, healing,
educating, and inspiring the people. His influence is heavily moral/philosophi-
cal, something that is much more important and yet much less visual than the
typical superhero preoccupations.

Jesus is not here to save us from immediate physical threat, such as several
miles of California west of the San Andreas Fault falling into the sea (*Superman*),
but from moral disintegration and eternal death. The superheroes are really glo-
rified human beings with special athletic, martial, and mental powers, but they
don't have any depth that surpasses human understanding, or any way to "save"
humanity in other than an immediate material sense. They are, to use biblical
language, gods made in our own image. The scope of the way in which Jesus
saves puts the accomplishments of the superheroes in proper perspective. And
the best part is that Jesus really was, is, and shall be.

8. God the Father and *The Godfather*

A friend of mine recently contracted a passionate regard for Francis Ford
Coppola's film *The Godfather* (1972). So strong is his partiality that he has decided to go and make disciples of all men and women for this "greatest film
ever." I saw the film more than a dozen years ago and was not eager to see
it again. I dislike watching bodies being periodically peppered by bullets (or

strangled, exploded, and so forth), regardless of the quality of the surrounding acting, but I decided to watch in the name of friendship and education.

If you have seen the film, you will remember that the godfather, Vito Corleone (played by Marlon Brando), is the elderly head of a New York family crime syndicate. By the end of the film Vito is dead and his son, Michael (Al Pacino), has become the new godfather. I once again found the acting, cinematography, and music impressive, but could not find the story very worthwhile, other than in remarking how the godfather's kingdom is a humorless parody of God the Father's.

The godfather lives in a palatial estate, surrounded by (mostly) loyal operatives ready to run to the ends of the earth (New Jersey, Las Vegas, Hollywood) to carry out the master's bidding. Somewhat like God, at least as represented in the book of Job, his business consists of listening to a daily report of problems and opportunities brought forward by his chief counselor and of rendering Solomonic decisions, which are immediately implemented by his operatives.

Again *somewhat* like God, on special occasions he entertains petitioners who come with prayers for assistance in personal or business matters. With considerable financial and political influence, the godfather is often able to carry out his will in a cordial, even charming manner, but when thwarted, he resorts to terrorizing his enemies into submission or rubbing them out.

The essential difference, which leads to many others, is that the godfather's kingdom is built on selfishness, while God the Father's is built on love. The godfather's kingdom preys on its subjects, creating and exploiting their vices for profit: gambling, prostitution, alcohol, and drugs. It is this larger evil that supports the "good" of its fine houses, clothes, cars. A privileged few (the "family") live high on the misery of others. God's kingdom, it need hardly be said, is based on a generous invitation to all, and the plan of salvation is built around God sacrificing Himself and His Son for the good of the masses, not the other way around.

Let me add something further about the difference between treating all others well, as a matter of principle, and treating only selected family members well. It is true that the godfather treats some of his relatives and associates well, kisses them on the cheek, offers encouraging words, does favors for them. But this is only as long as they are in his favor and as long as they keep on promising to do favors for him as he requests. Furthermore, those outside this favored circle are subject to any kind of reprehensible treatment, and those inside never know when they might suddenly be cast out.

The godfather's kingdom is pragmatic, and any means to a desired end is acceptable. Characters frequently lie to each other to gain a tactical advantage for plotting murders and other unsavory acts. For instance, Michael tells his brother-in-law, Carlo, that he's not going to get in trouble for confessing his part in the setup of Sonny. He tells Carlo that he will be extended grace. Once the confession is obtained, however, Michael immediately has his brother-in-law strangled.

Even though family loyalty is occasionally touted as a virtue in *The Godfather*, it is readily dispensable when it conflicts with self-interest. The cryptic tagline "It's nothing personal, just business," is used to excuse and even justify every kind of heinous action. In contrast, God the Father's kingdom is idealistic, based on principle. Ends can be accomplished only through means that do not violate those ends.

In the short term, the godfather's way of doing business appears dramatically effective. Michael is able to arrange the assassinations of his immediate rivals and consolidate power. (In a scene of great irony, the assassinations occur while he is acting as godfather at a dedication of his nephew and affirming his adherence to religious creed.)

However, not unlike Macbeth, Michael finds (as is further born out in *The Godfather, Part II*) that the seat of power is never secure, and he descends into a pitiful paranoia, all his good qualities and potential destroyed by his loss of character. The tragedy of the film is that old Vito supposedly entered a life of crime in order to become a better provider for his family, but that choice leads instead to the moral degradation of the family and the loss of character of his prized son and heir.

God the Father, it seems to me, has it right after all. The godfather makes "an offer we can't refuse," while God, on the other hand, makes an offer we can refuse—but after revisiting this film, I appreciate the opportunity to be a part of His family more than ever.

9. *Sister Act* and *Babette's Feast*

Let's say you were to ask me "What do the films *Sister Act* and *Babette's Feast* have in common, and what can we learn from them as Seventh-day Adventist Christians?" Here's what I might answer.

As a good Adventist, I like to lurk 10 or more years behind the cutting edge of culture, so I recently watched *Sister Act* (1992) for the first time. On the other hand, I've seen *Babette's Feast* (1987) so many times that I know the names of the quail, so let's get down to business.

Somebody once said that there are only two plots: a stranger comes to town, and somebody goes on a trip. Of course, for a stranger to come to town, he or she must first go on a trip, so sometimes the two plots are combined.

In *Sister Act*, Deloris (Whoopi Goldberg), a lounge singer, witnesses a mob-related murder and must get out of Reno to avoid being permanently silenced. A police detective arranges for her to hide out in a San Francisco convent, where her worldly-wise cynicism bumps up against the nuns' secluded innocence. From the nuns' perspective a stranger comes to town; from Deloris's, someone goes on a trip.

In *Babette's Feast*, two elderly sisters watch over a small flock of "brothers and sisters" in an ascetic religious community on the coast of Jutland, Denmark. Their pure but mundane lives take a turn when they accept a refugee Frenchwoman, Babette, as a cook. Thus, a stranger comes to town.

Both films have a special interest to Adventists, I think, because they present the encounter between a person from "the world" with special artistic talents and a conservative religious community. The interaction of the "worldly" artist and the religious community forms the central interest of both films.

Are you still with me? If so, let's glance at the religious and spiritual implications of each, starting with *Sister Act* (whipped cream) and finishing with *Babette's Feast* (cheesecake).

Deloris has a tough time dealing with plain food, silence, and a Spartan room at the convent. But her experience is turned around when she is given charge of the choir. Here is something she knows how to do: teach singing and choreography. In a ridiculously short time, she brings a powerful talent out of the nuns, and their Motown/gospel hybrid ("My Guy," changed into "My God") becomes the talk of the town, putting a lot of butts in the pews, as Deloris phrases it.

In a classic Adventist angle, there is high tension between conservative "purity" and using worldly techniques to appeal to a secular target audience. In the end, there is an ideal combination of music and spirit of worship (according to the logic of the movie), by which worldlings are drawn in and the pope, a special guest at the climactic performance, gives his full blessing.

What can be learned from all this? Deloris helps reestablish the "street cred" of the church, and so the church and the community are reintegrated. Good. Deloris gets the nuns excited about performing their best for God's glory. Good. Deloris learns about unselfishness and service from the nuns. Good. In the final danger scenes, where the mob is chasing Deloris through a casino, Deloris puts herself in harm's way in order to protect her "sister" nuns, showing a selflessness that demonstrates notable growth from where she was at the beginning of the movie. Good.

Some viewers may be uncomfortable with how Deloris uses a prayer for the opportunity to give two assassins a double punch in the groin, whereas others may object to the use of Motown style as an aid to the gospel. Nevertheless, I think the film is done with a spirit respectful of religion and religious persons and is worth watching once or twice—well, once.

Babette's Feast is a more serious film, without (at least for me) being any less engaging. It does an excellent job of raising questions about the connections and tensions between bodily and spiritual appetites. I remember back to my undergraduate days at Pacific Union College, some 20 years ago, when there was considerable debate on campus about whether the large amount of money that had been raised to buy a Tracker organ for the college church should rather be spent in building mission churches. Was the organ merely a wasteful pleasure of the senses, or was it the highest way of making a tribute to God?

It wasn't an easy question to answer back then, and I don't think it's easy when Babette spends 10,000 francs on one big blowout dinner. But if we take seriously Jesus' approval of Mary's extravagant gift of perfume and foot washing, we have to consider supreme and costly artistry as a worthy value, given the right conditions. In the case of *Babette's Feast*, the value does not disappear with the food on the plate. Rather, the dinner serves as a healing balm for the community and raises the sisters' ideas of spiritual development to a whole different level.

You might take another look at these films and see what you think. By the way, the story of salvation has the same two plots: a stranger comes to town, and somebody goes on a trip.

10. *Super Size Me*

"Everything's bigger in America. We've got the biggest cars, the biggest houses, the biggest companies, and finally, the biggest people." Thus begins narrator Morgan Spurlock in his documentary *Super Size Me* (2004). For the film, Spurlock goes on a 30-day exclusive McDonald's diet which, combined with no exercise, causes the initially healthy filmmaker to gain 24.5 pounds. Among other negative effects, his body fat percentage rises from 11 to 18, his cholesterol jumps 65 points, he suffered from headaches, depression, and major mood swings, and he temporarily doubled his risk of coronary heart disease. The film provides a dramatic and memorable message about what Americans are doing to themselves by their dependence on fast food.

Despite the widely known damage to health caused by a fast-food diet, every day in the U.S. one in four Americans patronizes a fast-food restaurant. According to statistics cited in the film, more than 60 percent of American adults are overweight, about 60 percent get no statistically significant exercise, and obesity is gaining on smoking as the number one preventable cause of death in the country.

But does this have anything to do with Adventists? We have had a strong health message and emphasis for more than a century. We have a tremendous worldwide health work, a vegetarian tradition, and a longtime stance against alcohol and smoking. We were even featured in *National Geographic* as one of three focus groups with unusual longevity (November 2005). On the other hand, an Adventist-run company manufactures America's number one sugar-filled snack cake, and how many of us, after all, live up to our health potential?

In almost 20 years of working on an Adventist university college campus I have witnessed many students compromising their health, whether it is going to bed too late, eating on the run, skipping breakfast, or having too much Sam's chicken (with tartar sauce). I could go on. I have some bad health habits myself, with love of cheese as a particular weakness.

Since I never eat at McDonald's anyway and go to the Adventist McDonald's (aka Taco Bell) only about two or three times a year, eating at fast-food restaurants is not my problem. But as with many important issues, we shouldn't stop with avoiding the bad. It's interesting to me how the Ten Commandments state negatives, as in "Thou shalt not kill," whereas Jesus reframes them as positive: "Love your neighbor as yourself." (Yes, I am aware of the interpretation of the commandments as positive promises, as in "You won't kill anyone," but that is still a different focus from the positive loving your neighbor.)

Turning this principle to diet, it's good to stop frequenting fast-food joints, but what about going beyond that and turning toward treating your body as a temple of God?

To refresh our memories, 1 Corinthians 6:19, 20 reads "Or do you not know that your body is a temple of the Holy Spirit who is in you, whom you have from God, and that you are not your own? For you have been bought with a price: therefore glorify God in your body." There's plenty of inspiration potential packed in these lines.

First, the Holy Spirit is dwelling in us. My wife likes us to keep our house tidy (and for that I'm thankful), and when we have company over, such as last night, she makes an extra effort to create an attractive and welcoming environment. I watched her out the window before the company came, going out to the backyard and cutting some fresh flowers for the table—the extra touch to beautify the environment for the guests.

Partly by the food we ingest, we create an environment for the Holy Spirit to inhabit. Or maybe it would be more accurate to say that by the food we ingest, we enhance or diminish our sensitivity to the Spirit.

That point about being bought with a price also hits home. I know that when I buy or make a nice gift for someone, I like to see them use it, enjoy it, take care of it. And when I think of the immeasurable gift Christ has given us, first, just life itself, but on top of that redemption, and when I think of the price He paid for it, it does indeed inspire me to want to take special care of His purchase.

Then there's the long term. It's so hard for us to think long term instead of short term in a society that is constantly telling us "90 days, same as cash." But if I live to be 70 or 80, I'd like to have a quality of life that is uncompromised by the bad health choices I could be making today and tomorrow. I'd rather have my children telling their children, "Let's go play golf with Grandpa tonight," instead of "Let's go see Grandpa on the respirator at the nursing home." And if that means eating rice and lentils for lunch instead of lasagna and a slice of cream cheese pie, bring on the lentils.

Getting back to *Super Size Me*, as with a number of artifacts of popular culture, I find it inspiring but incomplete. I'm glad that Spurlock did the film. I think it's worth seeing, and after viewing it I was personally inspired to live more healthfully. At the same time, Spurlock's perspective on the purpose of health is limited when compared to a Christian perspective. Learn from it what you can (which should be quite a bit), and work out for yourself how the health message of *Super Size Me* fits in with a bigger concept of health that is out there for the Christian.

Here are a couple of inspiring and insightful quotes to get started on.

"Those foods should be chosen that best supply the elements needed for building up the body. In this choice, appetite is not a safe guide. Through wrong habits of eating, the appetite has become perverted. Often it demands food that impairs health and causes weakness instead of strength. We cannot safely be guided by the customs of society. The disease and suffering that everywhere prevail are largely due to popular errors in regard to diet" (Ellen White, *The Ministry of Healing*, p. 295).

"Grains, fruits, nuts, and vegetables constitute the diet chosen for us by our Creator. These foods, prepared in as simple and natural a manner as possible, are the most healthful and nourishing. They impart a strength, a power of endurance, and a vigor of intellect that are not afforded by a more complex and stimulating diet" (*Ibid.*, p. 296).

"Abstemiousness [moderation] in diet is rewarded with mental and moral vigor" (*Ibid.*, p. 308).

11. Narnia

I entered Narnia late in life, as a master's student at Andrews University looking for new Sabbath afternoon reading. Each bite-sized chronicle took two or three hours to devour and didn't have the bad aftereffects of Turkish delight, so I read through them a number of times in the next 20 years, by myself mostly, but also aloud with our firstborn and with a C. S. Lewis class.

Although Narnia doesn't compare with Tolkien's Middle-earth as a fully realized imaginative world, the books are very entertaining, well-written, good company, fun on the lighter side. One doesn't want to be always plodding toward Mordor. I also appreciated the spiritual insights in Lewis's series, as in Eustace Scrubb's dragon phase in *The Voyage of the Dawn Treader*, and the redemption story via Aslan's sacrifice for Edmund in *The Lion, the Witch and the Wardrobe*.

So, having reread the book, I eagerly headed off to Chicago for a preview of the new Disney/Walden Media production of *The Chronicles of Narnia: The Lion, the Witch and the Wardrobe*. After all, if there are going to be seven years of this series, I want to know if the cows are fat or lean.

The book itself begins quietly, with the four Pevensie children—Peter, Susan, Edmund, and Lucy—heading off to Professor Kirke's house in the country to avoid the air raids in World War II London.

The film, in contrast, opens to high drama in the cockpit of a German bomber dropping its load as the children and their mother race for a backyard underground shelter. With crisp cutting and bombs detonating in surround sound, the filmmakers reassure us that we are here for spectacle, not some piddly old BBC production.

Additional invented backstory shows elder brother Peter tussling with Edmund, who has dashed back into the house to retrieve a picture of his father (away fighting the war). Edmund's retrieval of the picture nicely sets up the brothers' competitive relationship, which eventually contributes to Edmund's betrayal of his siblings.

There's also a clever match between the cracked picture frame that holds the photo of Mr. Pevensie and a later shot of Mr. Tumnus's father's portrait after Tumnus's house has been ransacked by the queen's secret police.

In short, the opening sequence does some of the good things a cinematic adaptation can do. Although staying true to the tenor of the book, it rewrites and adapts to develop the characters and to make things more visual, more cinematic. Even a mundane ride over a dirt road in a horse-drawn cart can create goose bumps when filmed in the right lighting from a dolly with a rising crane.

There are a number of other good things about the film. The casting of and acting by the children is excellent, particularly with Lucy (Georgie Henley) and Edmund (Skandar Keynes). Lucy is very sweet without being conventionally pretty or sentimentalized; she has an engaging smile without Hollywood teeth. She effectively expresses wonder, delight, and disappointment and even gets off some decent comic lines. Edmund is quite convincing in his consecutive roles as sneaking little traitor and born-again hero.

The outdoor landscape shots are breathtaking, which could be expected when you can take your pick of locations from New Zealand to Czech Republic. There are lots of nice tracking, crane, and aerial shots—you can compare how this film handles the train-carrying-main-characters-passes-through-lovely-countryside sequence to the same sequence in 50 other films and see that *Narnia* does it pretty well.

And of course the sets, the CGI (computer generated imagery) creatures, and the wardrobe (the costumes and accessories as well as the title piece of furniture) are excellent, almost up to the high standards set by *The Lord of the Rings* series.

Douglas Gresham, Lewis's stepson, was a consultant on the film and even has a bit part as a radio announcer in the opening sequence, giving the film an authentic Lewis tie. The film is quite faithful to the book, although one little sequence jumped out as a possible exception.

After Aslan's secret deal with the witch to exchange his life for Edmund's, Lucy approaches the solitary lion. In response to a question from her, Aslan says something such as "there is a magic more powerful that rules over all of us," which could imply that he is not a supreme being, merely another—albeit especially powerful—creature. However, it can be taken as just showing that "God" plays by the same rules as His creatures.

Even though *Narnia* is a well-made movie, in following *The Lord of the Rings* I think it suffers by comparison. I say this as one who is at least as much a fan of Lewis's writings as of Tolkien's. Tolkien's created world (in the books and on film) has more depth and consistency, much higher gravitas. Each *Rings* movie is longer than a football game.

I was amused to hear of a colleague who had a *Rings* party last year at which guests watched the whole series in one sitting, about 12 hours. That was too much of a good thing for me, but this length is well used by Peter Jackson and company, with more space devoted to character development, while not omitting spectacle. *Narnia* is not short—at two hours and 15 minutes—but it doesn't develop its characters in the way that *Rings* does.

Narnia (movie and book) has an odd menagerie of animals, freely mixing those from our world with mythical creatures, leading to anomalies such as polar bears (in springtime) drawing the witch's chariot into battle alongside Minotaurs and ogres, and on the good side centaurs and unicorns teamed up with cheetahs and rhinoceri. I'm not quite sure whether to expect Aslan or Marlin Perkins around the next corner. Middle-earth sticks with woodland and Northern European mythic creatures, which go together, and the incongruities of *Narnia* are more jarring on screen than in print.

A few more words are in order about the difference between book and movie experience. Lewis names a number of the species that surround Aslan on the Stone Table, and refers to "other creatures whom I won't describe because if I did the grown-ups would probably not let you read this book." The chummy re-

77

lationship between narrator and reader doesn't translate to film, nor does the book's ability to stimulate the reader's imagination. Film literalizes. Every creature must be created, down to the last bone and muscle, and no matter how well Weta Workshop does the job, some of us still like to imagine.

Lewis himself, in his essay "On Stories," says that "nothing can be more disastrous than the view that the cinema can and should replace popular fiction," because "there is death [to the imagination] in the camera." Whereas in books, the author's and reader's imaginations work in partnership, in film the viewer sees the representation of the imagination of another.

Furthermore, although film can operate at both the subtle and spectacular level—some fine close-ups of Lucy's changing expressions illustrate the former—spectacle causes a more immediate reaction, and seems to sell more tickets. Why else does every movie ad on TV seem to have the same scenes of door-opening-to-blazing-gun, car-or-body-crashing-through-large-window, and woman-starting-to-slip-out-of-sweater? Personally, my nerve receptors shut down when these clichés appear, but the people who promote and make movies are still way too attached to fireworks.

In *The Lion, the Witch and the Wardrobe*, for instance, there's an invented scene (not in the book) in which the children cross a river. The ice is breaking up, and they have a dramatic confrontation with a wolf pack. The wolves are snarling, the ice is cracking, Peter is waving his sword around, the frozen waterfall shatters, and the burst of water hurtles everyone downstream.

Technically it's an interesting scene, but emotionally it left me cold, just so much machinery calculated to push my anxiety buttons. Danger-on-the-ice-floes was really gripping back in *Way Down East* (1920)—partly because it climaxed two hours of really slow action, but also because a lot of groundwork had been done to make the viewer care greatly about the two characters out on the ice floes.

But this is not just a film to discuss in its aesthetic and technical aspects. It's being reviewed here partly to discuss its spiritual angle. "Is this a film," you ask, "to which I should take my unchurched son/neighbor/dentist?" Let's not place limitations on the Holy Spirit, but humanly speaking, *Narnia* does not portray a moving religious experience on the order of, say, *Places in the Heart, Babette's Feast, A Man for All Seasons*, or even *It's a Wonderful Life*.

There's something about thundering hooves in surround sound that is inimical to the contemplative setting often conducive to authentic religious experience. In that respect, Lewis's original story far outstrips the movie. One can follow the impulse to lay down the book and think about Aslan's sacrifice on the Stone Table, rather than being dragged across the sky and back into battle.

It's interesting to compare the small part the graphic description of the battle takes in the book to its expanded role in the movie. *Narnia*, I think, works better as a pretty well-made entertainment film than as something to applaud for profundity or spiritual insight.

After a big display of earthquake, wind, and fire, God speaks to Elijah in a still small voice (1 Kings 19). *Narnia* does a good job with the fireworks but falls short of this deeper, quieter level.

12. The Hills Are Alive With Adventists (*The Sound of Music*)

I must have been about 9 years old the first time I went to see *The Sound of Music*. Up to that point I had developed as a culturally normal Seventh-day Adventist. I recognized all the actors' voices on *Your Story Hour*. I had read *Brush Valley Adventure*; *Dookie, Sookie, and Big Mo*; *Singer on the Sand*; and all the Sam Campbell books; and I had *Swift Arrow* practically memorized: "I love you as a brother, Swift Arrow; I cannot marry you, for I love White Rabbit. Somehow I must become White Rabbit's squaw."

But my normal development was about to be interrupted. On that fateful Saturday night, our family packed into the Volkswagen for the drive from Loma Linda to La Sierra. I dimly remember anticipating something about singing children, which would not of itself have excited me, but this was clearly going to be a big event, and I might as well be in on it. It was not to be. We arrived at the parking lot to an ongoing murmur of consternation. I don't remember if the projector had broken, or the reels hadn't arrived, or what, but there was some such fiasco sufficient to cancel the showing. We drove home in dudgeon, without even entering the auditorium.

I'm not sure how I continued to miss seeing the film over the next decade. I did see *The Love Bug* three or four times. I could measure my burgeoning adolescence in the transference of interest from Dean Jones and Buddy Hackett to Michele Lee. I saw *The Yellowstone Cubs* a couple of times and all the Stan Midgley and Don Cooper movies. I fell asleep during *A Man for All Seasons*. Even though I hadn't seen *The Sound of Music*, I was absorbing it out of the very air I breathed. "Do-Re-Mi" was part of the basic music curriculum.

It wasn't until college that I actually saw Maria and company hiking across the silver screen. It was Sadie Hawkins reverse weekend at Pacific Union College, and I was invited to *The Sound of Music* by a hardened veteran of a couple dozen encounters. I felt like the last passenger pigeon in the sites of a collector, von Trapped. She brought popcorn and sang all the songs. I thought the movie was reasonably entertaining, but I was left wondering, *What's all the fuss about?*

The years have slipped by. I've seen the film several more times, and I've seen my children watch the film. A number of years ago, our then 4-year-old went through a three-month stage in which he insisted on being called Friedrich, and insisted on calling his mother and me Fraulein Maria and the captain. He insisted that he was 14, and told his teachers at preschool to call him Friedrich. I was beginning to fear that this phase might be permanent, until it was replaced by a new and consuming interest in pirates.

You don't have to take my word for it—you can probably trust your own experience—when I tell you that the *The Sound of Music* is at the heart of Adventist cultural literacy. Of all the films ever made, ahead of even *Ben-Hur* and the complete Walt Disney set from *Old Yeller* to *Treasure Island* and *The Computer Wore Tennis Shoes*, *The Sound of Music* holds a special place in our cinematic heritage. It is *the* film we all hold in common.

"Climb Ev'ry Mountain" was the class song for the 1968 graduates of Laurelwood Academy. It was also the class song for the 1968 graduates of Grand Ledge Academy. "Climb Ev'ry Mountain" was probably the class song for a lot of other academies in the late 1960s. When the first Adventist showing of the film in Colorado occurred at Campion Academy in 1969, people drove from across the state to attend. The gym was "packed to the rafters," according to one observer, for the most successful senior benefit in memory.

At the Andrews University premier, Adventists who wouldn't go to see the film in a theater drove down from Toronto on Sabbath afternoon to swell the hallowed halls of Johnson Gymnasium. People from all over Maine drove to Atlantic Union College for the showing, and when the sound system went out, the audience supplied the music from memory. One of our friends at Andrews University remembers a vacation in New York where she talked her father, an Andrews professor, into taking her and her brother to a showing of *The Sound of Music* at a theater. Her mother wouldn't go because if there had been a fire in the theater, she "wouldn't have been ready."

The previous generation knew where they were when John Kennedy was shot. My generation knows where we were when we first saw *The Sound of Music*. I asked the question of my Argentinean wife, a latecomer to the American cultural scene: "March 1974, Glendale Academy," she replied without hesitation. And it's not just a film that many of us have seen. It's a film we've seen again . . . and again . . . and again. One of my students told me that even before her family owned a VCR, every December her mother would rent a VCR and a copy of *The Sound of Music* for a family showing.

Some Adventists would no doubt rather have a more subtle and intricate film as our church's central cinematic legacy—perhaps something such as *The Seventh Seal* or even *Jesus of Montreal*. The fact is that we have *The Sound of Music*. Why? Some reasons apply to any audience for the film.

The film has a lot to offer children—it gratifies several of their central fantasies. First of all, children are tremendously important in the film. They are seen and heard—and appreciated. As the stars of Captain von Trapp's party, they sing "So Long, Farewell" to a group of admiring guests. They win over the baroness by crooning "The Sound of Music." ("Georg," she says, "you never told me how enchanting your children are.") The children put on a wonderful puppet show, and they top off their accomplishments by winning first place at the Salzburg Folk Festival. The typical child who watches the film can thrill to imagining themselves just as talented and appreciated as these screen children.

Furthermore, the children are cute, friendly to each other, and abundant—growing on trees, to adapt an image from the film. All of us who worried about crooked teeth or acne, who fretted about having no one to play with except one "dumb little brother" or sister, can bask in 172 minutes of raised self-esteem, sibling perfection, and plenitude.

But even from a child's point of view, the film does not exist in a pure state of naive wish fulfillment—a sufficient cloud on the horizon allows the wish fulfillment to pass the suspension of disbelief. The children's mother died several years earlier, and their father is encased in a shell of stern repression. Enter Fraulein Maria.

One of Freud's more fruitful discussions, in my opinion, describes a supposedly universal phenomenon he calls the "family romance." In the family romance, children reach an age in which they begin to see deficiencies in their

81

parents and begin to compare their parents with other parents, real or imagined. Not surprisingly, children are able to imagine better parents than their own: in material possessions, character, talent, community prestige. And they align themselves with these imagined parents by supposing themselves temporarily misplaced children, out of their real home, who will someday be rescued when their "real" parents return to claim them. There are many examples of this fantasy being played out in literature: in Dickens' novels, for instance, or in the children's classic *Nobody's Boy*. One might say that Christianity itself is based on a celestial family romance in which God, the perfect Parent, rescues us out of this vale of tears and takes us to our heavenly home.

A strictly terrestrial version of the family romance takes place in *The Sound of Music*. Having had only the shadowiest of mothers and a distant father, the children are virtually orphaned before Maria marches through the gates singing "I Have Confidence." This replacement fairy-godmother mother can magically make play clothes out of old curtains, sing enchanting songs, and, most important, make the children feel and be enchanting themselves—"Is there anything you can't do, Fraulein?" asks Baroness Schraeder with veiled sarcasm. Not only is Maria perfection herself—she brings the captain around. In one of the more sentimental scenes—I found myself torn between tearing up and gagging when I reviewed it the other day—the captain's heart melts when he first hears the children singing. He joins in the chorus, and then awkwardly embraces them all afterward. Thus, the children are elevated from an essentially dysfunctional home to a perfect one. This is an imaginative pattern that many children devour.

From a parent's point of view, the film supplies two obvious lines of attraction. First, we have good wholesome entertainment for our children. The story is pretty well innocent, sanitized, uplifting, etc.—only the puppets drink beer. And second, kids like it. Parents know how unusual this combination is, and they treasure it. Finally, parents of my generation can look at the film nostalgically as a reminder of their own childhood.

But perhaps there are some more particularly Adventist reasons we watch the film. It is certainly full of motifs we find familiar. I don't want to insist too much on the apocalyptic flight to the hills in the face of unwarranted persecution. After all, this time it is the Catholics fleeing the Nazis, instead of the Adventists fleeing the Catholics, an irony we should appreciate; but what Adventist child hasn't at one time or another daydreamed about that always imminent flight?

I remember being captivated by a book about the Waldenses as a child, all their adventures hiding out in the hills, and, if my memory serves me correctly, occasionally fighting back and vanquishing their opponents. I also read *Flee the Captor* a few times and knew, in my imagination, every cranny of the rock face John Weidner descended while the frustrated Germans cursed from above. I thought about what kinds of canned goods I'd like to take on our flight, if and when the time should arrive. Fleeing to the hills was part of the topography of my Adventist imagination.

But more obviously and perhaps more convincingly, the film taps into our repressed desire for song and dance. As Adventists, we have forbidden all uniform movement, except for Pathfinder drill marching—and note how we excel there. I am not trying to make an argument for academy sock hops, but inside some Adventists lurks a Fred Astaire or Ginger Rogers, all dressed up with nowhere to go. We want to sing and dance, to perform in musicals, even if they seem dumb and sentimental.

When I was at Loma Linda Academy, we had a class party with "folk marching," a euphemism for square dancing. Many of us had never really moved in a patterned way to music before, and we found it so enchanting that five or six of us signed up for square dancing lessons at a local mobile home park. We spent the next eight Tuesdays do-si-do-ing in a smoke-filled community room, while a caller with "Joe" emblazoned on his silver belt buckle called out the numbers.

The Adventist tension with song and dance is part of a larger tension we feel between the church and the individual, which the film also explores. I think there is a spiritual crossroads at which we feel we must strike out on our own, apart from the church, or deny ourselves and commit wholly to the church. Part of Maria wants to be a nun and part of her wants to live in the world, apart from the abbey. "How Do You Solve a Problem Like Maria?" ask the nuns; and many Adventists, who also feel a tension about their degree of commitment versus autonomy vis-a-vis the church, might ask, "How do you solve a problem like Maria's?"

Like many Adventists, Maria appreciates the church and wants to be a part of it—at times she longs for a self-annihilating commitment—yet both she and the mother superior doubt her fitness for such a commitment, and in many ways Maria does seem unfitted for the strict abbey life. For all it offers in terms of community and spiritual aura, the church can also be overpowering, oppressive. Many younger Adventists, I suspect, are not "Seeking a sanctuary," to use Bull and Keith Lockhart's rubric for Adventism, so much as seeking some kind of mediation between the sanctuary and the world. Cinematographer Ted McCord created a special dark-to-light transition when Maria leaves the abbey walls to go to the captain's house, and that feeling of being out from under watchful eyes censuring our movements is shared by many Adventists and ex-Adventists.

Maria relishes freedom of movement and voice on the road, enjoys her new confidence, and delights in her sense of self as she faces life on her own, out of the shelter of conventional wisdom. However, when she comes face-to-face, up close with the captain during an Austrian folk dance, she flees back to the abbey. She isn't ready to deal with the troubling emotional situations freedom brings.

Maria's resolution is one much desired by many Adventists. She lives out from under the abbey walls, yet has the approval, blessing, and friendship of her sisters. She is at peace with the church and herself, enjoying both community and individuality. This absence of dramatic tension, the harmonious integration of the different parts of her life, is to be expected as the resolution to a film.

In real life, however, we should expect and embrace a certain amount of ongoing tension. That's life. The most important factor in integration and balance, as I see it, gets little emphasis in the film. I'm speaking of the individual's relationship with God and our daily petitions for God to give us His Spirit and to help us balance competing demands, sort out choices, live wisely for the good of others. Whirling around a gazebo during a thunderstorm singing "I am 16 going on 17" is exciting and sustaining for a few minutes. Climbing across the hills to freedom makes a great final scene for a movie. But dancing with God, if you will accept the expression, can be sustaining for eternity.

13. *End of the Spear*

I watched *End of the Spear* last night. It's a 2006 film that, as you may know, tells the story of five missionary men who were killed by Waodani tribespeople in Ecuador in 1956. Subsequent to their husbands' deaths, several of the missionary widows go forward in witnessing to the Waodani, and succeed in winning many to Christ. In particular, the film focuses on one of the Waodani, a man named Mincayani, and the son of one of the men Mincayani speared.

The story line has great elements of Christian experience going for it: the commitment of the male missionaries, the bravery of their wives, the transformation of lives by God's grace. It's the kind of story I'd like to jump behind and give a full-fledged plug—but there are enough little problems with the artistry of the film to prevent my doing that.

The musical score seems intrusive and out of place, with continuous choral voices hyping almost every scene. The Indians' bodies look too gym-sculpted (see especially Louie Leonardo as Mincayani) to be believable, and the Waodani women wear knee-length skirts and massive vine-crafted bras (for lack of a better term) to make the film more family friendly, but these contradict documentary footage from the time. And the dental condition of the movie version Indians is marvelous.

Add to this the ambiguous "bright lights" scene at the end, which seems to represent either the souls of the murdered missionaries ascending to heaven or heavenly beings watching over the dying missionaries—it's safe to say that some kind of supernatural visitation is implied but not clarified—there are at least a half dozen ways in which the filmmaking gets in the way of the story. Not to say that this is a bad film. I would call it a decent to good film that missed a chance to be great.

In reading over the comments of Amazon reviewers, another point came to mind. When a film is "Christian," it's held to a slightly different standard than a secular film. Well, not exactly. A weak musical score is just weak, whether in a Christian film or not. But let's just say that any artistic weaknesses also reflect on the Christianity behind the film. That's why it's so important, as Christian artists, to do everything as well as we possibly can, as what we do reflects back not just on us but on our faith and, ultimately, our Creator.

I respect and appreciate what the team that put this film together was trying to accomplish. And I don't have answers for some of the difficult problems the film faced. For instance, you can't film the native women both modestly and authentically: what do you do? You want to convey the violence of the story without showing any "R" type violence on screen: how do you do that? You want your film to have crossover appeal (to a secular market), but have it also work for the home crowd. Some careful balancing has to take place, and some armchair critics (like me) will say that the balance didn't work.

All we can do, as Christian artists, is do our best and leave the results with God. I love Ellen White's quote about Jesus' reaction to His public: "In the heart of Christ, where reigned perfect harmony with God, there was perfect peace. He was never elated by applause, nor dejected by censure or disappointment" (*The Desire of Ages*, p. 330).

I'd like to end on a positive note about the film. In the final scene the missionary son flies off into the horizon with Mincayano (the man who speared his father), after coming to terms with loss, anger, and forgiveness. He says, "Through the years, people could always identify with our loss, but they could never imagine the way that we would experience gain." It's a profound insight, one of those Christian paradoxes that can bounce around in your head for hours, one more example of how God can make all things work together for good (Romans 8:28).

14. *A Man for All Seasons*

I was a kid the first time I saw *A Man for All Seasons*, and I fell asleep. It went right over my head. In the course of my last three or four viewings, however, it has become a personal favorite. I'm a little late jumping on the bandwagon, as it won six Academy Awards in 1966, including Best Picture. Being so old, however, it may need an introduction for the modern viewer.

The film concerns a controversy between Sir Thomas More and King Henry VIII. King Henry is childless and wishes to divorce—or rather, to have his marriage to Catherine of Aragon annulled—in order to produce a "legitimate" heir. Sir Thomas stands in his way. Although More reluctantly accepts the marriage (via an act of Parliament), he will not sign a further act that makes Henry VIII supreme head of the Church of England, superseding the pope's authority. In the end, the film focuses on the difference between those who value integrity—and are willing to give their lives for it—and those who do not.

Several elements combine to make this film a superlative treatment of the concept of integrity. The casting and acting are superb, the screenplay has marvelous dialogue (this was originally a play), and I could go on about the filming. But for purposes of this book, I want to stick with integrity.

At the beginning of the story, Sir Thomas is safe. He has friends, including the king and the Duke of Norfolk, a loving family, a comfortable household. He also has opponents and hangers-on. He's in a mixed situation, like a lot of us, with a series of assets and liabilities. As the story continues, however, his assets briefly rise, then steadily decline as his friends desert him, he is imprisoned, his family questions his sanity, and finally he is tried in a sham trial and executed.

His "friend" Rich wants to be good, but even more he wants to be at court, in the halls of power and activity. He spurns the opportunity to become a teacher away from the temptations of court. More, who offers him the teaching post, tells him that he could be a fine teacher, "perhaps even a great one." Rich replies, "If I was, who should know it?" To Rich, it seems quixotic to do good simply for the sake of doing good. Throughout the rest of the story, Rich steadily ascends in his gowns and positions, but at the cost of his moral and spiritual nature.

Likewise with More's good friend the Duke of Norfolk. Norfolk is More's sincere well-wisher, and urges More to capitulate with the king's wishes as a purely practical matter. Norfolk cannot understand one who will not bend a little "for convenience's sake."

Finally, More's own family comes to him in prison, and his daughter, perhaps the person More respects most, urges her father to "say the words of the oath and in your heart think otherwise." More rebuts her with one of the striking speeches of the film: "When a man takes an oath, he's holding his own self in his own hands . . . like water. And if he opens his fingers then, he needn't hope to find himself again."

More remains true to self and goes to the chopping block. This film gives the viewer the opportunity to ask "Was it worth it?" and reevaluate the price they put on integrity. I would call this a great film because it shows how precious integrity is, while it makes bending to convenience seem odious. At the same time, it shows how costly it can be to maintain integrity in the midst of a morality of convenience. It seems like a good time to bring out that golden quote of Ellen White from *Education*:

"The greatest want of the world is the want of men—men who will not be bought or sold, men who in their inmost souls are true and honest, men who do not fear to call sin by its right name, men whose conscience is as true to duty as the needle to the pole, men who will stand for the right though the heavens fall" (p. 57).

In the film, and presumably in real life, Thomas More was one of those men (or persons). That being said, it is only fair to point out that some aspects of More's life (not shown in the film) remain open to question. For instance, can we support his hostility to the Wycliffe translation of the Bible, or his support of the pope as the supreme leader of Christ's church on earth, or his antagonism to Luther and his followers? And following things another step, can we support Luther's anti-Semitic writings? No way! It just goes to show the difficulties we get into when we try to make a hero out of man. Thanks be to God that, as Christians, we have allegiance to a trinity of beings who are truly worthy of worship.

Passages to consider: Matthew 2:2; Matthew 4:10; Matthew 14:33; Romans 1:25; Revelation 14:7.

15. *The Dinner Game*

Have you ever called anyone an idiot? It can be momentarily satisfying to float up to your pedestal of superior humanity, looking over your nose at the cowering imbecile below you. Watching the French farce *The Dinner Game* (1999), however, might give you a new respect for (not) using that word.

A group of snobbish men hold a dinner each week, with the requirement that each bring an "idiot" as a guest. The snobs encourage the idiots to blab on about their special interests, such as boomerang throwing, meanwhile laughing up a storm behind their backs.

For the next dinner, Pierre Brochant invites Monsieur Pignon, a friendly and unsuspecting tax man, who has a hobby of building models of monuments with matchsticks—his Eiffel Tower required 346,422 of them, as he tells anyone who will listen. However, shortly before the dinner, Brochant strains his back, and his doctor tells him that he must cancel, stay home, and rest. He is too late to reach Pignon, who is coming to his apartment before the dinner, and Brochant's wife, who hates the meanness of the idiot dinner idea, goes out so as not to meet the candidate for humiliation. Thus the stage is set for an evening-long encounter between Brochant (the snob) and Pignon (the idiot).

Through a series of coincidences and mistakes in the farce tradition, Pignon ends up completely scrambling Brochant's affairs, including alienating Brochant's wife even further from her husband, providing unintentional revenge for the laughs the snobs have gotten from previous idiots. If the film stopped here, it would be a typical, amusing farce.

However, in a climactic scene Pignon, who has discovered that he was to be the amusing idiot at the dinner, rejects revenge and shows compassion instead. He calls Brochant's estranged wife and explains to her how he felt when his own wife left him two years earlier, how he turned to building matchstick monuments as a way of dealing with grief, and how he wouldn't wish such loneliness and emptiness on anyone, even someone who has labeled him an idiot and set out to make fun of him. In short, Pignon reconciles the couple with humanity, compassion, tact.

The film dramatically embodies some important truths. First, when we call others idiots, it is only a matter of time before the tables are turned and we're the idiots. Second, by giving derogatory labels to people, we blind ourselves to their full humanity, limiting ourselves to a caricature version of reality—which makes us the dummies. Third, calling other people idiots cuts us off from the vital quality of compassion. At the beginning, people such as Brochant, who have no compassion, may be witty, amusing, and sophisticated, but they don't make very good friends, much less spouses. They're certainly not going to be of any help when you need it. Only when Brochant becomes the idiot and feels what that's like, does he acquire the humility and compassion we would want in a true friend.

Hopefully, next time we're tempted to call someone an idiot, or even think of someone that way, we'll take a step back and get our compass recalibrated. By doing so, we can save the world from having to deal with one more idiot.

Passages to consider: *Matthew 5:22; 1 Corinthians 3:18.*

16. *Places in the Heart*

Places in the Heart (1984, director Robert Benton) has one of the most thrilling and inspired final scenes of any movie I know—but in order to talk about it I have to go over a few things that happen earlier in the film.

The story treats the inhabitants of a small town in Waxahachie, Texas, during the depression of the 1930s. At the beginning of the story, the Spalding family sits down to dinner. Mr. Spalding, the local sheriff, is called away from the table to handle a disturbance down by the train tracks. A young Black man has gotten drunk and is waving a pistol around. Tragically and accidentally, Mr. Spalding is killed by the young man, leaving Mrs. Spalding (Sally Field) a widow with two children. As payback, the town's White citizens lynch the shooter and drag his body through the streets behind a truck. Mrs. Spalding is appalled at this act. She is encouraged by the local banker to sell her land, as she won't be able to meet the mortgage, but being a woman of strong spirit, she determines to grow and sell sufficient cotton to pay the mortgage and hang on to the land. A subplot treats the adulterous relationship of Mrs.

Spalding's brother-in-law (Ed Harris) and the local schoolteacher.

As Mrs. Spalding doesn't know beans about cotton, she hires a Black share-cropper, Moze (Danny Glover), to superintend her efforts, and takes in a blind boarder, Mr. Will (John Malkovich), for the meager rent he will pay. In the end, through backbreaking labor, wit, and courage, she makes the money and pays the mortgage installment. The little team of misfits defies convention. If this were the whole story, *Places in the Heart* wouldn't be too different from a hundred other uplifting underdog stories. It's the last scene that makes it different.

We move inside the church, where the pastor is preaching on 1 Corinthians 13, after which the congregation takes Communion. The tray of Communion cups is passed to one character after another, as careful camera work keeps us from looking ahead. We see the tray passed to the adulterous husband. To his wife. To 12 more persons. To Moze. Wait a second—he has already left town. Gradually we realize that Blacks and Whites are together in church in a town in which they always lived separately. The Communion tray goes to the Spalding children, then to Mrs. Spalding, then to her deceased husband, who passes it on to the young boy who killed him. I remember a chill going over me the first time I saw this scene.

It's as if a veil is drawn back and we can see into another dimension, a spiritual reality that is there, influencing our world, but not easily palpable. The wife who has been cheated on could not forgive her husband under ordinary circumstances, but she takes his hand again under a dispensation of grace. Mr. Spalding can't be brought back to life. He can't pass the grape juice to the kid who shot and killed him. Moze, who was run out of town by KKK members, can't be there, calmly taking Communion. Not in this life. Not without God's grace.

But through God, all things are possible. That's why I love this film. It labors along in realistic mode for 90 minutes, then ends by shifting into another dimension, one that I believe is even more true and solid than the wooden desk in front of me. It's in that dimension that all my highest hopes and dreams are located. It's that dimension that offers grace, redemption, and community in the way God intended things to be, recovered from the waste and hopelessness of sin. I love *Places in the Heart*, because it shows me that dimension in action—real, credible, incredible.

Passages to consider: *Ezra 9:7, 8; John 1:16; Romans 5:20; 1 Corinthians 15:10.*

17. *Luther*

One of the important questions raised in the movie *Luther* (2003) is "How are we saved?" Johann Tetzel, the Commissioner of Indulgences for Germany (played by Alfred Molina), promotes the idea that salvation is for sale, through the church. That idea is still at least dimly reflected in the televangelist programs that flash 800 numbers for contributions after soul-shaking messages. The young Luther (Joseph Fiennes), on the other hand, tries to find salvation in endless confession of his sins, but the more he confesses, the more guilty and condemned he feels, admitting that he lives "in terror of judgment."

A turning point occurs when his father superior talks with him. First, he tells Martin that "arguing with the devil never does any of us any good. He has had 5,000 years of practice. He knows all the weak spots." In response to Martin's query as to how he can find a God of love, his superior replies, "Bind yourself to Christ and you will know God's love. Say to Him, 'I am Yours; save me.'" It's a moving scene, combining good theology with compassionate action— Martin's mentor models Christ's love with his own, bending down to embrace the suffering monk.

Another issue of importance is access to and study of the Bible. Luther worked very hard to produce a translation of the New Testament into German. In a fine scene near the end of the film, Luther presents a bound copy to his patron, Prince Frederick the Wise (Sir Peter Ustinov). Notice the way Prince Frederick's fingers flutter as Luther steps forward to present the gift. It indicates the precious quality of God's Word, the inestimable privilege of having the Bible in one's modern tongue. Would that we would be filled with more of Prince Frederick's trembling excitement each time we take up God's Word.

Luther himself was deeply immersed in God's Word. The story is well-known about him praying on the Lateran staircase in Rome, when the words "the just shall live by faith" (Habakkuk 2:4) came to his mind. Throughout Luther's life, the study of God's Word had a vital impact on how he lived, thought, discussed. In several scenes, *Luther* shows the title character debating and discussing with others, using God's Word as a resource for truth.

One final point from the movie concerns the Peasants' War of 1524 to 1525. Although the movie is not too clear on the origin of the war, it seems that some of the peasants took Luther's disagreements with church authorities as licensing across-the-board social upheaval. As Luther observed the mayhem and murder, he was sickened and called for the nobility to use all necessary force to suppress the rebellion. I was impressed with the devil's ingenuity in turning something good (at least in part) right back to evil. The devil has many avenues to lead us away from God, and he is completely open-minded about leading us down any of them. For instance, if sitting in church but not attending to the service or allowing God to work on our hearts is where we are at, the devil will plump the cushions, so to speak, to keep us happy there. On the other hand, if we get roused up against complacency or status quo in the church, he will be pleased to push us toward fanaticism, lack of charity, impatience, anger. The only thing he can't abide is having us draw closer to Christ and leading others to the Savior. Luther, though not by any means a perfect man, did work very hard to bring others to Christ. Thankfully God can use imperfect tools—like Luther, you, and me.

Passages to consider: 2 Corinthians 12:9; Ephesians 6:10-18; James 4:7.

18. *Enchanted April*

Enchanted April (1992) has long been on my admired films list. It's one of those so-called women's movies that focus on intimate relationships, rather than a bunch of men shooting off weapons, planning an elaborate jewel heist, and driving recklessly through the streets of a major metropolitan area.

The story features two middle-class Englishwomen, Lottie and Rose, who plan a dream getaway from their predictable and disappointing lives—a month renting a small medieval Italian castle. They invite two other women, Lady Caroline Dester and Mrs. Fisher (who respond to their classified ad), to join them and share expenses.

Rewatching the film, I can't help but think that it illustrates some important things about the differences between heaven and earth. The English scenes, which begin the movie, are brown, dull, rainy, metropolitan, crowded. The personal relationships are superficial, irritating, selfish. Lottie's husband can think only about business; Rose's husband writes romance novels under a pseudonym and flirts with a much younger woman. Lady Caroline, with her good looks and fortune, is the center of the party, but longs for escape from a world in which men are always hovering and grabbing. Mrs. Fisher is isolated and lonely, the pictures on her mantel of days gone by as her only companions. The English scenes, in short, show the weaknesses of fallen humanity and the drab and depressing life that surrounds fallen beings.

Then the women travel to Italy, in this film a sort of heaven on earth. It's raining and nighttime when they arrive—a final nod to England—but the next morning when Lottie opens the shutters, a beautiful vista appears. The castle is high on a hill overlooking the sea. The water sparkles. Birds sing. The *Enchanted April* oboe motif kicks in. The warm light gives color to Lottie's flesh. She sees Rose leaning over a bunch of flowers, intoxicated by their scent. The women laugh at and with each other, dazzled by their magical abode.

Little by little a transformation works through all four of them, starting with Lottie, who spreads a spirit of love and generosity to the rest. After a few days, following her deepest impulses, she decides to invite her husband, Mellersh, to join the women, even though he was part of what she was escaping from at the beginning. "It would be mean not to share all this," she explains to Rose. She goes on to clarify her new insights about love: "This place makes me feel flooded with love. The important thing is to have lots of love about. I was very stingy with it back home. I used to measure and count it out. I had this obsession with justice, you see. I wouldn't love Mellersh unless he loved me back exactly as much. And as he didn't, neither did I. The emptiness of it all."

Mellersh responds to Lottie's invitation, and although his first impulse, on arriving at the castle, is to make a splendid business project out of his fortunate introduction to Lady Caroline, he too becomes enchanted with a new spirit of generosity and kindness, and he and Lottie truly love each other for the first time. Rose and her husband have their own transformation, and Lottie and Mellersh draw old Mrs. Fisher into their circle of warmth. Finally only Lady Caroline, used to being at the center of everything, is left alone.

The story provides an inspired twist, with Lady Caroline coming to love and be loved by Mr. Briggs, the owner of the castle the women are renting, who stops by to visit. Mr. Briggs, who loves the oboe, has weak eyes as a result of a war injury. He sees Lady Caroline only as a haze that, ironically, works wonders for both of them, allowing him to know her without the distraction of her beauty, and allowing her to know that Mr. Briggs cares for her according to her inner qualities.

A weakness in my analogy of heaven and earth, Italy and England, is that in the film earthly characters are placed in "heaven" and then begin their transformation as a response to the heavenly atmosphere. We cannot book passage for heaven in the same way that they can head off to Italy, but we can begin experiencing the spirit of heaven as soon as we let God give it to us. What a transformation that will make in our present attitudes and relationships!

As the couples leave "San Salvatore" to return to their ordinary lives, they believe that they can carry the enchanted spirit with them. As a final gesture, Mrs. Fisher plants her walking stick in the ground and, over time, it magically grows buds, flowers, leaves. It's the culminating example of transformation, from something dead to something beautiful and alive. It is a heavenly transformation, the kind God will most willingly work in us day by day.

Passages to consider: *2 Corinthians 3:18; Philippians 2:13.*

19. *Romero*

On March 24, 1980, Monseñor Oscar Romero, Archbishop of San Salvador, the capital city of El Salvador, was assassinated. His story is told in the 1989 film *Romero*, directed by John Duigan and starring Raul Julia. Romero was killed, so it seems, for standing up to the ruling class on behalf of the peasants of El Salvador.

The film portrays Romero as a reticent and bookish man, a peacemaker, but one who will take a stand, speak out against injustice, and put his life on the line for his beliefs, if the situation calls for it. The film raises important questions about the degree to which the church should be involved in politics.

In El Salvador, in the period leading up to Romero's death, the government wanted the church as an ally in order to perpetuate the status quo—a small wealthy elite and an enormous mass of peasants. The government (and the army supporting it) wished the church to act, in Marxist terms, as the opiate of the people, getting the poor to focus on loving their neighbor and trusting in heaven to rectify the injustices of earth.

The more radical priests of that time were involved in liberation theology, bringing social justice to the poor here and now, on this earth. In extreme cases this included using armed force to aid the cause. Romero, as portrayed in the film, wanted to bring social justice to all—though of course the poor, as most sinned against, would experience the most change in their situation if social justice were to occur. However, he sought to achieve such justice only through peaceful means.

The thing that most impressed me in the movie is how much power accrues to someone who is not afraid to die. The intimidation tactics of the military and the government depended on the fear of the masses. When a few, such as Romero, stood up against this intimidation, yet without parallel violence, they acquired a moral force that in many cases overwhelmed the military's arsenal of machine guns and prison cells.

Of course, it is possible to give up your life for an evil cause, as in the case of suicide bombers—and note how much influence for bad these people have. How much better to imitate Romero's willingness to put his life on the line for the right cause. Romero did not seek death, and no doubt, all things being equal, he would have preferred not to be a martyr—to have that cup taken from him. I don't want to be a martyr either. But I pray that God will help me know what is worth dying for and, as will more likely be an issue for each of us, what is worth living for on a day-to-day basis.

Passages to consider: *Psalm 37:5; John 11:25.*

PART 3: More Culture

1. Extreme Irony

A recent issue of *Sports Illustrated* reports on some of the latest entries in the field of extreme sports. Extreme ironing supposedly "combines the adrenaline buzz of surfing with the satisfaction of a well-pressed shirt." The accompanying photo shows a participant in high-tech gear atop a rocky pinnacle with standing space the size of a hula hoop, ironing away as the dizzying landscape drops off on all sides.

For those less fussy about their clothes there is mountain bike bog-snorkeling, in which enthusiasts ride into a bog on lead-shot-weighted bicycles and use snorkels to preserve respiration as they circle a marker with their heads underwater before returning to land.

A third new sport involves chasing a rolling cheese down a hill and trying to catch it. Despite injuries to a number of contestants, one cheese chaser says, "If you can't get completely blotto and hurl yourself down a hill in pursuit of a Double Gloucester, what's the point of living?"

As a lover of cheese, I have some sympathy with this contestant. Were cheese a wild animal that required pursuit and capture, I could conceivably end up racing down a hill after it and risking a crack on the crown for my efforts. But as there is plenty of subdued and shrink-wrapped cheese at the local grocery, I will save my strength for contemplating these extreme pursuits.

It intrigues me that people can put so much energy, creativity, athleticism, time, and risk of bodily injury toward something that most people would consider to be patently absurd. Is this extreme irony? Presumably that's part of the motivation for participants: identity apart from the mass.

These are not people who shop at Wal-Mart and watch Rosie O'Donnell.

And compared to the socially acceptable absurdity of working one's way up the corporate ladder, living on the hill, and driving a Mercedes/Porsche/Jaguar/Escalade, there's something innocent, whimsical, engaging, and selfless about throwing oneself after a tumbling cheddar.

These must be interesting people. Wouldn't you rather spend a half hour with a passionate bog-snorkeler than with, say, a Raiders football fan? (Note to my brother and other Raiders fan friends: I'm speaking of a Raiders fan in the abstract, not you, with your many endearing qualities.)

So I admire these extreme athletes for their creativity in coming up with new pursuits, their desire to participate, and the absence of the trappings of professional sports. Perhaps these sports represent healthy recreation. Perhaps extreme ironing should be categorized with stamp collecting as an innocent pastime, a refreshing activity for those with sufficient leisure and inclination who want to push the envelope.

Truth be told, many of the rest of us have avocations that lead us to occasional absurdities. Confessing my own case, studying and performing "standards" from American popular songs has led to a fondness for "Mr. Sandman." But there's more to life than the thrilling harmonies of the Chordettes. There is a difference between a pastime and a purpose.

A book that describes some of the new extreme sports has an instructive title: *100 Things to Do Before You Die.* This title admirably captures a potentially dangerous direction of these (and our own less dangerous) pursuits: the idea that there is no sufficient megapurpose to life, so we must amuse ourselves as best we can in the brief time allotted. The title *Sports Illustrated* attached to the relevant report echoes this philosophy: "Chairmen of the Bored."

Surely Christians should never be among the bored, and not just because we share the usual (or extreme) amusements of our society. Instead, we ask God to teach us to number our days so that we may present to Him a heart of wisdom (Psalm 90:12), including a wise use of that most precious gift: time. May we have the creativity, energy, and sense of humor of these extreme sports enthusiasts, but attached to a higher purpose.

And by the way, which of us is going to get started on writing *100 Things to Do After You Die?*

Passages to consider: *John 17:13; 2 Peter 3:13, 14.*

99

2. Gentlemen Lite

What is a "gentleman"? In the Victorian era, the term was associated with owning inherited property and being of upper-class birth. It also had attributes one could acquire, such as a good education (attending Oxford or Cambridge—much easier if you inherited property) and character: not only having good manners, but manners motivated by care and consideration for others.

In the United States, we can be glad that we have had less of the property and birth limits, but we can hardly be said to have uplifted the term "gentleman." I won't waste time discussing "gentlemen's clubs," a first-class oxymoron when applied to strip joints. Instead, I'd like to take on a (slightly) less degraded usage, that of *GQ*, aka *Gentlemen's Quarterly*, or, as I would rename it, *Gentlemen Lite*.

As I leaf through an issue of *GQ*, I see one small element of the traditional gentleman foregrounded: style. Page after page, "gentlemen" are defined by what they wear—and their scraggy little beards. And what do *GQ* men wear? Ridiculously expensive clothes, such as an $830 belt by Prada and a $145 pair of Levi's jeans. *GQ's* motto is "Look sharp. Live smart." Whether it *is* smart to buy a belt that costs more than 2 billion adults on our planet will earn in a year is apparently not under consideration, and I have a hard time giving *GQ* IQ points for fashion tips such as "You don't have to wear a belt with jeans, but if you do, try a military-inspired canvas one with leather army boots for a progressive look."

GQ is a conflicted magazine, trying to preserve a certain moral tone while pushing all-out consumption. On the one hand, the issue I am perusing has a well-written article condemning the flourishing sex trade in Costa Rica. On the other hand, Cameron Diaz in a bikini top ($290 from Dolce and Gabbana) is pictured on the cover to sell copies, and most of the photos in the accompanying interview emphasize her as an object to ogle. *GQ* is condemning the sex trade in Costa Rica and simultaneously exploiting it at home.

In a "*GQ* Promotion," an unholy mix of ad (mostly) and copy, a Hanes T-shirt is touted as providing "immediate access to cool." *GQ* sells cool, which, for many, apparently, is a satisfactory substitute for joy. None of the models look happy or joyful in the expensive clothes they are wearing. If I were to supply one adjective each for the first 10 faces in ads they would be "serious, somber, thoughtful, absorbed, stoned, pouty, pouty, stoned, self-absorbed, and kneel-down-and-worship-me-right-now."

I believe that a Christian ought to look decent—not just having clean finger-nails, but clothes that fit well and look well—to a point. *GQ* has that point mag-nified and expanded *way* out of proportion and, to my eye, that makes the resulting "gentleman" a travesty, a horror.

Ellen White has a few things to say about gentlemen, including this quote for teachers, which naturally caught my eye:

"Every teacher and every professor in our conference work should pre-serve the characteristics of the Christian gentleman when associating with his students. He should show himself a friend, a counselor. He should be tender, noble, benevolent, and truly courteous. When all our ministers cultivate the spirit of Christian gentlemen, they will find access to hearts; ears will be open to hear, and souls [will] be softened to receive the light beams of truth" (*Manuscript Releases*, volume 20, p. 186).

I like this quote because it emphasizes the character definition of gentle-man, and it gives a purpose for this character: to make us more effective co-laborers with Christ.

So farewell to Cameron Diaz, the "complete wardrobe for under $4,000," the "The Gods of British Rock," and all the pouty gentlemen lite in their Versace suits and Zegna cologne. By God's grace, we can be gentlemen (and women) with a worthy purpose, looking to make this world a better place, not just looking at ourselves in a mirror.

Passages to consider: *Micah 4:11, 12; Ephesians 2:10.*

3. Eddie Rickenbacker's World and Ours

When I was a kid, I read Eddie Rickenbacker's autobiography several times (*Rickenbacker: An Autobiography*, 1967). I thought he must have led the most exciting life ever. Among other things, he was a race car driver in the early days of the automobile, before World War I. During the war he learned how to fly and became America's "Ace of Aces" for shooting down 26 enemy aircraft (planes and balloons). After the war he started an automobile company, and later he became president of Eastern Airlines. During World War II he was in a plane that made a forced water landing on the Pacific. He and the crew sur-vived for 24 days on three lifeboats before they were rescued.

In addition to his numerous death-defying scrapes, Rickenbacker (1890-1973) lived through a tremendous age of changing technology. He was right there in the early days of the telephone, the automobile, the history of aviation, the invention of television. Rickenbacker saw it all. *Lucky bloke,* I thought. He *lived through all these inventions, and now there's probably nothing more to invent.*

Looking back, 30-plus years later, I smile. In my last two years at boarding school, in the late 1970s, I remember how cutting-edge it felt to be using my English teacher's IBM Selectric typewriter with—*ta-da*—correctotype! For those of you who missed this, in the pre-correctotype days you had to . . . well, I'll save that story for when you're trying to fall asleep.

All through college I wrote my papers on an electric typewriter. When I started my master's program (1982), I got my first computer, a RadioShack model that had a low resolution black and white screen, and no hard drive. You used 5.25? floppy disks for everything, and crashes were frequent, but it was an awesome improvement. I wrote my dissertation on such a computer and used a separate floppy for each chapter. Just as a curious side note, I calculated that I could put 142 copies of the manuscript *Screen Deep* on my date-sized 64 megabyte flash drive.

I will always remember the explosion of e-mail and the Internet, because it was happening around the time that our family lived in Argentina (1995), and we first used that technology to stay in touch with people back in the United States. Yes, Eddie Rickenbacker lived through a fascinating period of technological change that transformed his world—and so have I. The personal computer, the laptop, e-mail, the Internet, PDAs, BlackBerrys, cell phones, MP3 players, have all transformed our daily lives and our national culture to an amazing extent.

I'd like to take a few paragraphs to consider a couple of these inventions from a Christian perspective.

4. iPod

The first iPod hit the streets in 2001. The new iPods keep getting smaller, and each generation can do more—the latest wrinkle is playing video. Approximately 50 million iPods have (as of June 2006) been sold worldwide, of which two belong to the teens in our family.

How has the iPod, and its rival MP3 players (of which I own one), changed daily life? For starters, they feed three ravenous appetites of modern life: a highly personalized environment, immediate gratification, and massive possession of portable data. Let's take these one at a time.

When I was a kid, we didn't even have television. Yes, television was generally available, but our family didn't own a set—until later. If I wanted to see a movie, I went to the "Adventist theater" at Burden Hall on the Loma Linda University campus, where once in a while on Saturday nights they would show a Disney movie, or possibly have Stan Midgley in person with one of his comic travelogues. These were big community events, and I can still remember the whirring noise of the projectors and see the big reels of film as the technicians loaded them up.

Down the road a bit we got a television, and we went to fewer community gatherings as we congregated around the household screen. It amazes (and depresses) me to think how exciting it was when my parents first let me stay up to watch *Hogan's Heroes* with them in black and white. In my later teen years we got multiple televisions so that nobody's viewing preferences would cause conflict with anybody else's.

Musically, it was a similar story. I grew up hearing classical broadcasts of FM and occasional big-band recordings that my father liked. There was one system for the house. I didn't have any personalized musical experience until I got a little transistor radio as a teen and was able to listen to popular music and Dodgers broadcasts in my bed at night.

Think of the enormous difference created by the iPod and its imitators. You can now have a library of thousands of your exclusive favorites. You can arrange them into as many different playlists and classifications as you like. And—this is a big one—you can listen any time because you have headphones.

In many ways I like this. As a music lover, I like listening, I like listening to what I like, and I like listening while I'm tooling around the house cleaning the kitchen, folding laundry, jogging, whatever. My wife, who shares some but not all of my musical tastes, appreciates having quiet instead of the Red Garland Trio. Everyone's a winner, right?

Well, let's look at the other side. For all that the iPod has contributed to individual experience, it has taken away from community. Everyone has noticed, no doubt, how the ear-budded person in public seems to exist inside a little layer of clear plastic wrap. You might make fleeting eye contact, but you don't speak. They are in a different world. It can get a little weird when you talk to someone with long hair and get no response; then they turn around and see your lips moving, and reach under their hair to remove their earphones. "Hey, were you talking to me?" I think the iPod phenomenon has made us less tolerant of community experience, more demanding of having our own way in larger and larger segments of our experience.

In our modern world we increasingly rub shoulders with people who are physically present but mentally absent from the space they are occupying. After every class I see students hastening into the halls to call back friends—they have been out of touch for up to an hour and a quarter, students slapping back their earphones, checking their text messages. It is harder for this generation—probably quite a bit harder—to be physically present and concentrating on any one thing. And I think we pay less attention to the people around us because we often wall ourselves off from them with our portable devices. Anything that has a negative effect on community is something for the Christian to consider seriously.

It's also harder for us to enjoy and appreciate silence, something we all need. With portable sound wherever we go, we have to make a deliberate choice to seek silence—we don't naturally experience it nearly as much as previous generations. And silence is vital to having any quality of thought, having downtime for our multitasking brains, and, especially, for communion with God. Remember the still, small voice (1 Kings 19:12)? The last thing we would want is for our lives to be so full that there is no room for God.

Let me recommend to you a beautiful poem by A. E. Stallings, "Extinction of Silence." You can find it on the Web, though it was originally published in *Poetry* (February 2006). Here are the first four lines:

"That it was shy when alive goes without saying.
We know it vanished at the sound of voices
Or footsteps. It took wing at the slightest noises,
Though it could be approached by someone praying."

Passage to consider: *Psalm 62:1.*

5. MySpace

A recent *Newsweek* features a cover story entitled "Putting the 'We' in Web," reporting on the newest wave in user-generated Web sites such as MySpace, Flickr, and YouTube. I thought it might be interesting to talk about MySpace alongside two other sites that exist, although they are not generally accessible. I have given them the fictional names SpySpace and HighSpace.

MySpace, currently touted as the most popular Web site in the United States, is a user-generated social networking site, where individuals can present their favorite music, post pictures and video of themselves, share their thoughts (or thoughtlessness) in blogs, and create a personal profile that shares as many of their likes, dislikes, and personal habits as they wish to share. If I wanted to join MySpace, I could broadcast a controlled version of myself to . . . well, anyone who wanted to check me out. This is just what excites some users, the chance to make cyber friends.

SpySpace is my chosen name for another profile of me (and you), or actually several, that exists in government and commercial data banks, based on Google searches, credit card purchases, and other observable behavior. I can guess at a few things that may be out there, but I really don't know what kind of profile "they" have of me, and I have only very limited control of what goes in there. Recently *The Atlantic Monthly* ran an article about the government's information gathering resources (April 2006), and it's amazing all the data that can be pooled about any particular person the government deems worth observing. For you readers of *1984*, the article is titled "Big Brother Is Listening."

Perhaps it's my generation, but I have no thirst for a MySpace site—I'd rather meet "friends" face-to-face—and I'm not too happy about other people out there collecting information about me for SpySpace. However, it's the third site I really want to talk about.

HighSpace (feel free to improve on this name) is what I'm calling the profile of me that is being collected and recorded in heaven. I don't know what it looks like, or how I'm portrayed. I know that its creators have no limitations on access to information. They will know, for instance, not only the things I've bought but all the things I've thought about buying. They will know that I didn't get around to preparing a card for my wife for our anniversary yesterday (not quite the unpardonable sin, but close). However, I did record a karaoke love song just for her, and we went out for lunch, followed by a walk overlooking the beach. It's all available at HighSpace.

Not only that. At HighSpace, they know the motives behind what I do, all my pettiness, selfishness, and other forms of idiocy. If they made my HighSpace profile public—well, let's just say that I'm glad they've got a good security system and a very well-thought-out privacy policy up there.

The only way you could feel good about someone else having so much information about you would be if you had complete trust in that person. In their wisdom, their discretion, their love. That's a bit too much to ask of any human being, although a spouse can come close. It's not too much to ask of God.

He can click on HighSpace, so to speak, and find out everything about me, and He still wants—even longs—to be my friend, and yours. By the way, He's got a pretty extensive blog Himself, starting with a riff called Genesis. We ought to read it some time and get to know Him.

6. The Gospel According to John

An issue of *ESPN The Magazine* ran an excerpt of the recent autobiography (*My Life in and out of the Rough*) of talented but troubled golfer John Daly. Daly, who won two Majors, the 1991 PGA Championship and the 1995 British Open, and several lesser tournaments, is noted for being one of the longest hitters in golf, as well as having a very good short game. His talent is first-rate. On the downside, "Long John" has had well-publicized problems with alcoholism; marriage (his fourth wife was recently sentenced to five months in a plea bargain related to money laundering charges); smoking; consuming huge amounts of diet coke, M&M's and Big Macs; and gambling (he claims to have lost $50 to $60 million). Indeed, Daly is a poster boy, of sorts, for living large.

As a sidebar to their profile, ESPN printed a page with "The Gospel According to John," random thoughts about life from this man of excess. I thought it might be interesting to juxtapose some excerpts from "The Gospel According to John [Daly]" and "The Gospel According to John" (in italics).

"The first time I came out of rehab, in 1993, I said I was never going to drink again. The second time I came out of rehab, in 1997, I said I would never say I was never going to drink again."

"Whoever drinks of the water that I will give him shall never thirst; but the water that I will give him will become in him a well of water springing up to eternal life" (John 4:14).

"If I was still drinking whiskey, I wouldn't be drinking anything right now. I'd be dead. That's the truth, and I know it. I drink beer. Miller Lite. Sometimes just a little. Sometimes more. And sometimes—not as often [as] I used to, but sometimes—too much."

"The thief comes only to steal and kill and destroy; I came that they may

have life, and have it abundantly" (John 10:10).

"One day back in 2005, I stepped on the scales and I was at 278. I don't know how I got there, but there I was . . . By the time the U. S. Open rolls around, I'll be between 220 and 235. That's why I have racks of pants in my closet running from 36 inches at the waist to 44 inches."

"My food is to do the will of Him who sent Me and to accomplish His work" (John 4:34).

"I am the bread of life; he who comes to Me will not hunger, and who believes in Me will never thirst. . . .The one who comes to Me I will certainly not cast out (John 6:35-37).

"My agents have busted their butts trying to throw a rope around me, but I don't listen. And until I listen, well . . . all I can say is, I'm going to have to start listening soon, real soon. . . In 1996, the whole cycle began again: up and down, back and forth, waiting for my quarterly checks to pay off the casinos, hustling appearance fees, running myself ragged doing corporate outings instead of spending time with my family and working on my game.

"That's the way it's been for the past 10 years. It worries me. A lot. My wife, Sherrie, has been very supportive. She tells me that the kids don't do without—and she's right. They go to great private schools. They have everything they need. They're set up just fine."

"I am the vine, you are the branches; he who abides in Me and I in him, he bears much fruit; for apart from Me you can do nothing" (John 15:5).

"Here's my plan [on how to get his gambling addiction under control]. Every time I go to the casino, I start with the $25 slots. Plus, I set loss number, and once I hit that number, I walk out. If I make a little bit, then maybe I move up to the $100 slots or the $500s or maybe I take it to the blackjack table. Why not try to double it?"

"If the Son makes you free, you will be free indeed" (John 8:36).

[When asked "Are you ever going to stop partying?"]: "Not until they turn out the lights for good."

"I am the Light of the world; he who follows Me will not walk in the darkness, but will have the Light of life" (John 8:12).

John Daly is not unusual in his problems, only in their scale. His live-for-today philosophy and the problems it has caused for him and his family should provide ample warning to any reasonable observer. But here's what I find fascinating and heartbreaking: he still wants to drink—just beer instead of Jack Daniel's—and he still wants to gamble—just not the $5,000 slots. He keeps playing with fire instead of fleeing from it. His predicament reminds me of Ellen White's ropes of sand passage from *Steps to Christ*:

"Your promises and resolutions are like ropes of sand. You cannot control your thoughts, your impulses, your affections. The knowledge of your broken promises and forfeited pledges weakens your confidence in your own sincerity, and causes you to feel that God cannot accept you" ("Consecration" chapter, p. 47).

Ellen White continues: "You cannot change your heart, you cannot of yourself give to God its affections; but you can *choose* to serve Him. You can give Him your will; He will then work in you to will and to do according to His good pleasure. Thus your whole nature will be brought under the control of the Spirit of Christ; your affections will be centered upon Him, your thoughts will be in harmony with Him."

Thank God and His mercy for the possibility of changed lives. May we all take Him up on His promises, His good news, the true gospel.

7. Muscle and Fitness

"Shocking Report: Pro bodybuilder gains 50 pounds of muscle in 42 days!" Underneath this headline is a picture of a man with short blond hair, carefully coiffed and oiled. He is frowning, and his fists are clenched in front of his abdomen in the "crab" pose. His pecs are incredible, suspended above his lower abdomen like misplaced buttocks. His abundant veins make his torso look like a yard with too many gophers. He is a sight to behold, the back cover advertisement to the latest copy of *Muscle and Fitness*.

As I leaf through the magazine, I try to process its operational definition of manliness: (1) a man is obsessively concerned with his appearance; (2) a man shaves his chest, arms, and legs, but keeps a constant stubble on his chin; (3) a man takes whatever supplements are necessary to whip his body into its greatest potential mass; (4) happiness (for a man) is being stared at for his "beautiful" body; (5) a man spends 90 percent of his time in the weight room training, 5 percent of his time eating his special diet, and the other 5 percent with his arms around one or two women at photo shoots.

As one who could not do a pull-up to escape a crocodile, you might consider me unqualified to critique bodybuilding. I accept your criticism, and promise to read your book when it comes out. Meanwhile, what do you do with your powerful pecs once you have them? Find excuses to walk through the mall in a tank top so you can get ogled? Cruise the beach wearing shades so you can monitor response? Sorry. No time for that—you've got to be training!

I'm asking myself why I'm so critical of bodybuilding? What's so different about spending hours in the gym sculpting muscle, compared to training for the cross-country team, practicing the violin, knitting? It's just a hobby like any other, isn't it? On the other hand, you're not encouraged to pour all kinds of chemicals into your body to become a better knitter. And when you play violin, you're drawing attention to the beauty of the music—or you should be—which seems morally different from drawing attention to the beauty of your body. When you train for the cross-country team, you're enhancing your fitness, not putting it at risk.

The bodybuilding mentality pushes one of the really dangerous ideas of the American way: bigger is better. It's not good enough to have adequate muscles for any physical task you might be likely to face; you must have muscles totally out of proportion to any physical tasks. And it's not enough to be big; you can always get bigger. I read a *Sports Illustrated* article about bodybuilding a few years back, which noted that, paradoxically, bodybuilders are some of the most insecure people regarding their body image. It said that they have so much of their egos tied up in their physiques that they're hypercritical of how they look, easily threatened by competing bodies.

Fortunately, washboard abs are not a requirement for the Christian. Good fitness, taking care of the temple of God, yes, those things are to be desired, but one of the Christian's most important characteristics is to have the different components of his or her life in balance and subordinate to the overall goal of serving God. As Paul writes, "Bodily discipline is only of little profit, but godliness is profitable for all things, since it holds promise for the present life and also for the life to come" (1 Timothy 4:8).

As Christians, we have to ask ourselves what we're spending our time on, especially our discretionary time, and see if it's apportioned according to our stated values. How is our desire to love God with all our heart, soul, and mind, and our neighbors as ourselves, reflected in the way we spend our time? May God give us the insight to answer that question well, and the self-discipline to make appropriate changes.

Passages to consider: *1 Corinthians 3:16, 17; 1 Corinthians 9:24-27.*

8. C28 Clothing

Matthew 6:28, 29 reads: "And why are you worried about clothing? Observe how the lilies of the field grow; they do not toil nor do they spin, yet I say to you that not even Solomon in all his glory clothed himself like one of these." This verse really spoke to me in college, along about the time I read *Walden,* by Henry David Thoreau. For those of you who haven't read this classic, it is the author's account of living the simple life in a 10' by 15' log cabin next to Walden Pond. It draws a contrast between the conventional, civilized life and a life that is much more elemental materially, but much richer spiritually (though not Christian). His critique on modern society seems as applicable today as it was then. Here are some of his meditations on clothes in the chapter "Economy."

"It is an interesting question how far men would retain their relative rank if they were divested of their clothes."

"No man ever stood the lower in my estimation for having a patch in his clothes; yet I am sure that there is greater anxiety, commonly, to have fashionable, or at least clean and unpatched clothes, than to have a sound conscience."

"I say, beware of all enterprises that require new clothes, and not rather a new wearer of clothes."

After reading Thoreau, who got along on one pair of "pantaloons," I decided that I could thrive on alternating two pairs of jeans, which I did for a few months. And since then, when I purchase clothes, I often feel Thoreau sitting on my shoulder urging, "Simplicity! Simplicity! Simplicity!" My original encounter with Thoreau, however, was a couple of decades before the advent of C28, "Your Source for Bold Christian Gifts, Christian T-shirts, clothing, and Jewelry!" according to their home page.

As I flip through the hyperlinks, I see T-shirts, belt buckles, wristbands, hoodies, bracelets, pants—typical fare for casual teen clothing. Dove earrings, anyone? How about a lanyard with the bold Christian message that "King Kong is not my grandpa"? Or a "Souldog" T-shirt for street cred?

The C28 refers to Colossians 2:8, which says, "See to it that no one takes you captive through hollow and deceptive philosophy, which depends on human tradition and the basic principles of this world rather than on Christ"

(NIV). An interesting text on which to base a clothing line. So which is it? Am I being taken captive by buying Tommy Hilfiger or by buying C28? Should I, as a Christian, make an effort to buy clothes from an up-front Christian clothes ministry? As always, the final judgment goes to God, but here are a few thoughts on the matter in the meantime.

Can clothes be Christian? Clothes generally have a functional purpose, of providing modesty and aiding retention of heat, or possibly giving sun protection. They can also have a statement function, as in Joseph's coat of many colors. But binaries are too simplistic. Clothes can also look attractive and modest, without boldly making a statement. C28 clothes are designed to look like typical teen clothes, to help teens blend in rather than stand out, except for the message: a Bible text, a fish symbol, an acronym such as NWOT, as in "not of this world," from John 8:23. They can be manufactured in China or India, or wherever it's cheapest to manufacture clothes, simply substituting a Christian message in the production process.

Overall, I like to avoid "branding" myself with clothes, whether it's a Nike baseball cap or, theoretically, a C28 hoodie. The branding idea is part of our modern advertising onslaught, and everybody gets tagged by the goods they buy and display. I'm particularly wary of this in a Christian context, because a shirt can't make you a Christian. One of the things I like about God's "army" is that there's no uniform. On the other hand, if someone wants to buy a shirt to reflect their allegiance to God, just as I bought a T-shirt at a double-bassist convention last summer, who am I to say no?

What is more inspiring to me, as a visitor to the C28 Web site, is the conversion story of the founder and other gospel-oriented print material, including the mission statement, "to glorify God by sharing the life-changing gospel message of grace, truth, and love found in Jesus Christ."

I am reminded of the story in which John complains to Jesus about someone casting out demons in the Master's name (Mark 9). Jesus replies "Do not hinder him, for there is no one who will perform a miracle in My name, and be able soon afterward to speak evil of Me. For he who is not against us is for us" (verses 39, 40). I don't plan to buy any C28 clothing, and I'm not attracted to the heavy metal Christian bands such as Seventh Day Slumber that they help sponsor, but then I'm not the target audience for C28. They are trying to reach secular young people and bring them to Christ, and if they can accomplish that through their store, I wish them Godspeed.

Passage to consider: *1 Corinthians 9:19-23.*

9. John Grisham's *The Testament*

Over the years I have listened to a number of John Grisham novels on audiobook, thanks to the services of our local public library. I read (or listen to) Grisham because he's a good storyteller, I learn quite a bit about the legal profession, and Grisham is generally interested in moral thinking, what constitutes right and wrong in the contemporary world. I don't always agree with Grisham, and some of his novels deal too much with the seamy side for me (such as *The King of Torts*), but others of his novels have very well-drawn positive characters, or characters undergoing positive moral change, such as the main character of *The Street Lawyer*, who finds new meaning in working for the homeless. I especially appreciate the moral perspective in *The Testament*, which I am currently listening to for the second time.

The "testament" in question is the will of one Troy Phelan, a billionaire. At the beginning of the novel, the terminally ill Phelan commits suicide, and the rest of the novel treats the contest over his will. Phelan has made a last-minute will that gives the great bulk of his fortune to an unknown illegitimate daughter, Rachel Lane, who is serving as a missionary among native peoples in a very remote area of Brazil called the Pantanal. Phelan's legitimate children—who throughout the story are portrayed as extremely selfish, immature, materialistic, and foolish—are contrasted with Rachel, who has no use for the trappings of civilized society, and finds it at odds with her desire to devote herself to God's service.

In the middle is Nate O'Riley, a lawyer in his middle 40s, who was a very successful litigator in his early career. However, he has been battling alcohol for a number of years and is in a rehab clinic for the third time as the story opens. He is part of the firm that is serving as the executor of Phelan's will, and the head of the firm assigns Nate to go to remote Brazil to find Rachel Lane and inform her that she is the heir.

Grisham creates a powerful and memorable contrast between the grasping legitimate Phelan children (and Phelan ex-wives, and all their lawyers) and Rachel Lane. He makes materialism, greed, and selfishness very vivid, loathsome, and sometimes comic, and shows in Rachel a strong and convincing contrasting example. Rachel is particularly noteworthy and unusual as a praying, believing, inspiring Christian authentically living out her values and not portrayed as a loony.

In between Rachel and the squabbling would-be heirs, as I said, Grisham presents Nate as someone who would be good but who is made very weak by his alcohol addiction and lack of moral orientation. Some of the most interesting passages of the story include Rachel's discussions with Nate about the values of his world and hers.

You might ask what the reward is in reading a story like this, which includes examples of greed, lying, poor parenting, and other negative behavior. For me, it lies in the overall moral perspective. Good and right behavior appear especially good and right when convincingly portrayed alongside its opposite. This doesn't work if the author is crudely didactic, but in this case I think Grisham does some of his most skillful work in the contrast. All the characters, including the rotten Phelan children, are looked at with a certain sympathy and compassion, and there is a good balance between taking "nurture" into account while still holding the characters responsible for their choices.

The Bible has lots of passages that contrast the views of "the world" and the Christian. We are warned that there is a basic conflict between the way "the world" thinks and the way God thinks, that the worries of the world and the things of the world can cut us off from communion with God (Mark 4:19), that to be fully realized beings we must break away from the world's mold and let God shape us (Romans 12:2). These are fundamental ideas that we need to understand better—through studying our Bibles and talking with God, certainly. But these are also matters about which John Grisham, in this book, can teach us something valuable.

And I haven't even mentioned Father Phil, the idiosyncratic cleric who becomes Nate's friend at the end—he's worth meeting.

Passage to consider: *Isaiah 29:23, 24.*

10. *Mountains Beyond Mountains*

Paul Farmer was born in October of 1959. I was born in March of the same year. He's the kind of person I look at and think, *Wow! He accomplished all that in the same number of years that I've been on this planet?*

I recently read his story in *Mountains Beyond Mountains: The Quest of Dr. Paul Farmer, A Man Who Would Cure the World*, by Tracy Kidder (Random House, 2003). Dr. Farmer is a physician, a graduate of Harvard Medical School, who also has a Ph.D. in medical anthropology. He is a world-renowned specialist in infectious diseases, particularly tuberculosis and HIV/AIDS.

During most of the past two decades, Farmer has had an unusual schedule. A few months a year he teaches at Harvard Medical School and works at the Brigham and Women's Hospital in Boston. The rest of the year he works in Cange, Haiti, at the clinic Zanmi Lasante, giving free medical care to those who cannot afford to pay—the vast majority of Haitians. Simultaneously, Farmer makes many trips to consult on other health projects he is involved in—in Peru, Russia, Rwanda, and other locations.

One of Farmer's signature phrases is "a preferential option for the poor," as in giving the poor high-quality health care whether or not they can pay for it. Early on in the book, the author muses that "the world is full of miserable places. One way of living comfortably is not to think about them or, when you do, to send money." Farmer has taken a different approach. He has dedicated his life to personally caring for others at a fraction of the monetary compensation he would receive from grateful patients in Boston.

Farmer reminds me in many ways of Christ, in the friendly way he interacts with all patients, combining medical expertise with generous personal warmth. Although he accomplishes a tremendous amount of work, he doesn't seem to rush, and enjoys talking with patients and getting to know them. He is able to put all kinds of people at ease by the warmth and genuineness of his personality, and he is able to use his considerable expertise to create great good among many patients.

I'm trying to put my finger on it, and maybe it's this. With his background in anthropology, Farmer is able to see the big picture, how the social policies of governments affect the larger population, but for whatever reason he also seems to have a wonderful gift for connecting with individuals. I think that was a defining characteristic of Christ: big picture, small picture, both in perfect focus.

It's wonderfully inspiring to see a person of such gifts using them in such an altruistic way. It helps me to say, "This is what following in Christ's footsteps means." If you have any interest in health issues or social justice, you will find this an engaging book.

I should mention that although Farmer works congenially with church organizations and clergy, he does not call himself a Christian or make proclamations of religious faith—at least not within the context of this book. In a few matters he is not a model of Christian behavior. But when I think about the judgment scene described in Matthew 25:31-46, I think there are few who would wish to change places with him. Farmer, in essence, is doing what the rich young ruler did not—valuing the poor over his possessions.

Passage to consider: *Matthew 19:16-30.*

11. The Persuaders, Part 1

I recently watched a fascinating *Frontline* show called "The Persuaders," about the persuasion industry, mainly in advertising, but also in politics. One of the most interesting parts was a segment on Clotaire Rapaille, a French psychiatrist who once worked with autistic children, but now works on helping Fortune 500 companies unlock the code, or "reptilian hot buttons," that will get the most money out of consumer wallets and into the hands of Rapaille and his clients.

Rapaille claims that he pays little attention to what consumers say; instead, he focuses on deciphering why they do what they do. The key to this, according to Rapaille, is to understand the operation of the "reptilian brain," which is much more powerful in consumer decisions than the logical brain or cortex. "I don't care what you're going to try to tell me intellectually," says Rapaille. "Give me the reptilian. Why? Because the reptilian always wins."

To discover the reptilian code, Rapaille works with consumers in group interviews, going through various exercises to plumb their collective subconscious. Thus, for instance, he discovered, while consulting for a French business that wished to sell its cheese in the United States, that in France cheese is considered to be "alive," and you wouldn't put your cheese in the refrigerator because you wouldn't put your cat in the refrigerator. In America, however, cheese is considered to be dead, and health is more important than taste. For Americans, therefore, it is important to have pasteurized, sealed cheese, "safe" cheese. Americans must be marketed to differently from the French.

Likewise with the Hummer and, generally, SUVs. The "code" for the SUV, according to Rapaille, is "domination," so it makes no sense to produce an eco-friendly, smaller version of the SUV. Its imposing footprint is its identity and main selling point. It assures the reptilian brain that the owner is safe and secure in its fortress.

I found Rapaille's insights interesting and disturbing. His discoveries have undoubtedly led to some marketing improvements for some of his clients, but has he really gotten at the truth? It would seem to me that the concept of the reptilian brain is an affront to God the Creator, who made us in His image. It reduces humans to complicated puppets for master manipulators such as Rapaille: press our hot buttons in the right order, and laugh as we whip out our credit cards.

Think about Rapaille, trying to find out about what is at the core of being human, then using that knowledge, so far as he can understand it, to manipulate people for his benefit. It's a devilish business. Contrast God, who, we are told, knit us together in our mother's womb (Psalm 139:13). He isn't trying to use focus groups to discover what we're like inside in our core being. He knows. Furthermore, He's not using that knowledge to manipulate us for His benefit. He gave up security and safety—in direct opposition to the reptilian brain, I might add—in order to save us.

I don't believe that the reptilian brain is at the core. The idea is repulsive to me and contradicts all my ideals, but those are not logical reasons to disbelieve it. Rather, I disbelieve because the reptilian brain undervalues the manifest spiritual nature and potential of human beings, the altruism that, while no means universal, is visible across cultures in many contexts. It also distorts the portrait of human origin and nature as portrayed in the Bible. In contrast with Rapaille, I don't believe that the reptilian brain is going to win in the end. Give me the mind of Christ (1 Corinthians 2:16) any day.

Passage to consider: *1 Corinthians 2.*

12. Persuaders, Part 2

Can brand identification replace religion? That's the question that struck me after listening to Douglas Atkin, a marketing executive and author of *The Culting of Brands: When Customers Become True Believers,* and Kevin Roberts, CEO Worldwide of Saatchi & Saatchi and author of *Lovemarks: The Future Beyond Brands.*

Atkin, a marketing specialist whose company has produced branding campaigns for Mercedes-Benz, JetBlue, Citigroup, BMW, and Pfizer decided that studying cults and the blind devotion adherents have to them would give him keys to create a similar beyond-rational devotion for a brand. So he interviewed, for example, people who watched WWF wrestling, Mac users, Volkswagen and Saturn drivers.

People who buy these products, according to Atkin, do so to join a sort of community of individuals with like values and to make meaning. The superbrands—think Apple and Nike—have a sort of philosophy and interpretation of the world, a meaning system, that devotees buy into.

For instance, Nike's long series of "Just Do It" ads showed athletes reaching transcendent levels through sport. Slow-motion images showed runners striding, weight lifters straining, flecks of sweat flying, expressions of determination, willpower, suffering, and joy—sport as spiritual experience, a sort of cult of the body, an alternate religion.

According to Roberts, "The brands that can move to that emotional level, that create loyalty beyond reason, will be the brands where premium profits lie." And Roberts coined the name "lovemarks" to indicate brands that have achieved this kind of loyalty: Nike, Starbucks, and so on.

As I thought about Atkin's and Roberts' ideas, I was struck by the poverty of a religious experience that could be replaced by Nike. After all, after all the hype, the music, the slow-motion photography, the athletic brilliance, what the consumer is getting is an overpriced box of shoes, or a chance to wear the same $90 polo shirt Tiger Woods wears (that the company gave him for free). Saturn may make decent cars, but considering other Saturn owners as part of one's extended family, attending, along with 45,000 other Saturn owners, a "family reunion" at the automaker's plant in Tennessee, proselytizing friends and relatives to become Saturn owners? I have a hard time justifying making a religion out of a horseless carriage.

Compare Nike to Christianity. Instead of the mythological goddess of victory, you get the living God himself, His best-selling book, and an invitation to a personal relationship with Him. That's real transcendence, and nothing on this old earth can compare with it.

Passages to consider: *Ephesians 2:19-22.*

3. The Persuaders, Part 3

Frank Luntz's specialty is testing words, finding the right words to sell a product or a policy. He uses focus groups extensively, and his special niche is using "dial technology" to register their moment by moment reactions to a particular message—participants rotate a knob on a little electronic device to show their ongoing reactions on a numerical scale.

Luntz is noted for getting the Republicans, for instance, to consistently use the phrase "climate change" instead of "global warming," and "death tax" instead of "estate tax." He has helped Rudy Giuliani, George W. Bush, and lots of other Republicans who want help selling themselves and their policies.

As a writer, someone who works with words all day long, I'm particularly interested to see how contrasting phrases can affect perception. I have learned how important it is to think carefully about word choice, to revise and revise again. But even though I share Luntz's concern for words, I'm not in his camp. His primary concern seems to be getting his client's agenda approved or accepted by the public, not whether what his client is trying to do is good for the public (though he also mentions this). It's a patronizing, manipulative approach.

For instance, while "death tax" is somewhat descriptive, it's a much more emotional construction than "estate tax," which, from Luntz's perspective, is just the point. He wants to grab people by their emotions, bypass their reason. Note how people on either side of an issue choose labels that predetermine the correctness of their side. It makes a big difference whether you are labeled as a "rebel" or a "freedom fighter," and how could anyone be against either "pro-choice" or "right-to-life"? The problem is, if we use these labels that have already decided the issue, we can't think through the issue, which is just what we need to do. Persuaders such as Luntz encourage emotional reaction rather than thought.

In this light, God's method of communication is pretty daring. He gave us an incredible book, written by lots of different authors, expressing their divine insights through widely different personalities. God's speakers aren't little robots—which is what the Republicans look like when you see them using "climate change" instead of "global warming" one after the other and you know that it's an agreed upon script.

God doesn't dumb down His message to a second-grade reading level. His statements are complex enough to challenge our professors of theology for a lifetime, yet simple enough to educate the humbler students. His most advanced servants are, by definition, the closest to Him, yet most fully individual. God always respects (and enjoys) individuality.

One other thing. We can believe—*I* certainly believe—that God alone can be trusted to consistently act in our best interests, something we can hardly expect from the persuasion industry.

Passage to Consider: *Luke 11:11-13.*

14. *T.H.E. Journal*

On the cover a little kid, probably 8 or 9 years old, sits on a bed, a laptop resting on his crossed legs. He's wearing Bill Gates, Jr., glasses, and he's chewing thoughtfully on one of his index fingers; his hair is tousled. I believe that we are supposed to translate this image as "profound thinker, executive of the future." God forgive me, but I really hate *T.H.E. Journal* (Technology Horizons in Education).

It's one of those unsolicited advertising publications, a 65-page paean to our supposedly inevitable enslavement to technology. Every page shows gleaming laptops, beaming educators bent over classroom multimedia stations, glowing anecdotes about distributed education (aka distance learning).

A few pages in, there's one of those student-studying-on-the-lawn pictures. The guy has glasses, a pullover, and a laptop. He's staring into the distance as if he just discovered relativity. The rest of the page displays a variety of laptops that, presumably, can help the rest of us unpack the atom.

Then there's the satiric ad that pictures dumpy old overhead projectors and snarls of cable, and asks the reader, "Do you really want to spend more on these?" Of course not, when there are gleaming, newer, faster, sexier, yadda-yadda-yaddas for a really reasonable price.

Oh-oh. Here comes the little multicultural no-child-left-behind ploy. A cute little girl in plaid shorts sits cross-legged in profile, the inevitable laptop on her legs. She turns questioningly toward the reader. Will you keep her supplied with brand-new Gateway computers or doom her to third-world status?

One ad features a red, a blue, and a green crayon, the better to connect us to the red, blue, and green software packages below. Another features rows of students looking at monitors—each lit up with a different colorful graph or table—while the smiling teacher stands in the front of the classroom with access to each student's monitor. The epitome of the "smart classroom."

Have you sensed that I have just a teensy-weensy problem with the idea that technology is going to save education, make us all marvelous teachers, and allow students to comprehend global culture and earth's history (available on a new three-DVD set) by the time they graduate, and that whenever a problem comes along we can just come up with a new gizmo-box and things will be better than ever?

OK, I'm writing this on a computer. I drive a car. I ordered two books and a CD over the Internet the other day. "Work on column for *Spectrum*" is on my Palm Pilot's to-do list. So I'm not running off to join the Amish, and how can I bite the hand that feeds me? Here's where I get off the technology train.

When technology gets put before people—especially when the technology is advertised as putting people first. Like your typical cell phone ad, which promotes the idea that you can be "with" someone wherever you are, while overlooking that use of a cell phone presumes a double absence: from the person with whom you are speaking and from your immediate environment.

When cutting-edge technology is presented as must-have. The 30-year-old Bosch mixer we got from my grandfather is still working great. I ride the bike I got in college, 20-odd years ago. Still fine. I play golf with 10-year-old clubs. The ball still goes straight if I make a good swing. My desktop computer is four years old. OK, it bites big-time, and I really need a new one. But overall I am not in a perpetual state of tech-deficit-depression, as the advertisers grabbing for my wallet would like me to believe.

When technology creates mind clutter. Keeping up with technology can be a full-time job. In the old days, how much time could you waste going out to the mailbox to see if the mail carrier had come? How much time can you waste today by constantly checking your e-mail or having your thoughts rerouted by a mail ding?

When technology is presented as a savior. Ads of every stripe are constantly presenting their product as "the savior." This would be harmful, of course, were we to believe it, but after a few years of such bombardment, another danger can arise: we get so cynical to the idea of false saviors that we forget that a real one exists. Christians, if anyone, should know a real savior when they see one. May God prevent us from both pitfalls.

Writing these Thoreauvian thoughts, I'm inspired to have a techno-free day, but I have to e-mail an article to a magazine, so I'll slake my spirit by tossing *T.H.E.* in the trash.

Passage to consider: *Luke 12:13-34.*

15. *Left to Tell,* **Part 1**

Left to Tell: Discovering God Amidst the Rwandan Holocaust (Hay House, 2006) by Immaculée Ilibagiza, is an autobiographical account of one young woman's experience of the genocide of 1994. As a student of language, I was particularly struck by the role language played in the anti-Tutsi genocide, and the role it played in Ilibagiza's salvation.

First, much of the divisive spirit necessary for the genocide was created by RTLM radio, the Hutu-backed radio depicted as Hutu Power Radio in the film *Hotel Rwanda*. The humanity of the Tutsi was attacked by consistently referring to them as "cockroaches" or "snakes" who must be "squashed" or "exterminated." The slaughter was legitimized by euphemistically referring to it as "work," as in, "Have you started to work yet?"—the routine morning radio greeting during the days of killing.

Ilibagiza talks about hearing, while in hiding, masses of killers chanting "Kill them, kill them, kill them all; kill them big and kill them small! Kill the old and kill the young . . ." The chanting was a way of creating team unity and a sense of righteousness among the killers. As I read this, I couldn't help thinking of James 3:5, which, when talking about the power of the tongue, or words, says, "See how great a forest is set aflame by such a small fire!" In short, *Left to Tell* provides a chilling account of the power of words to corrupt, to produce evil.

On the other hand, the author talks about the positive power of words. For 91 days she hid in the home of a Hutu pastor in a secret bathroom whose door was covered by a wardrobe. Crowded in a tiny space with up to seven other women, Ilibagiza began to pray—all day long. From the time she awoke she communed with God, spending hours contemplating the meanings of words such as "forgiveness," "faith," and "hope." She says that she spent days with the word "surrender," thinking about what it meant to give herself over to a higher power. In my mind's eye I can see Ilibagiza in her little cell, thinking on, say, "hope," while outside wild, murderous mobs swarm the streets looking for more "cockroaches," and I see the paths to heaven and hell that we are given in our use of language.

One of my father's favorite texts is Proverbs 25:11: "Like apples of gold in settings of silver is a word spoken in right circumstances." I want to use my mouth for good, not evil, but I also know that I have a tendency to put my foot in it, to blurt out things through selfishness, dimwittedness, lack of the right spirit. Thankfully, God has offered to help us with our speech. Let's join with the psalmist, who says, "I will guard my ways that I may not sin with my tongue" (Psalm 39:1).

16. *Left to Tell,* **Part 2**

Reading *Left to Tell*, I was reminded of Jesus' parable of the wise and foolish builders (Matthew 7:24-29), who built their houses, respectively, on rock and on sand. The buildings themselves may have looked identical, but when the great storms came, the difference was evident.

Likewise, many Hutus and Tutsis got along well enough in the pregenocidal days; in fact, there was considerable intermarriage between Hutus and Tutsis. It would have been unthinkable on March 31, say, a week before the genocide began, to grab your machete and go out to hack your neighbors to pieces. However, once the storm began, many—let us even say the great majority—either joined directly in the killing or expressed sufficient indifference to allow it to go on. These were people whose morals, whose sense of justice and fair play, and whose appreciation of human life were only skin-deep. On the other hand, a number of Hutus stood up for their Tutsi friends or for decent humanity in general, and condemned the killings, hid refugees, and did other things to counteract the violence. Many of them paid for their boldness with their lives. Nevertheless, they showed that their values went to the core of their beings, to rock, not sand.

For those of us who have not yet been tested in extreme circumstances, now is the time to prepare. God Himself has promised to be our trainer, and day by day He will help us shape our characters into something beautiful and strong for Him. I used to think something along the lines of *Well, what if the day of trouble doesn't come during my lifetime? Will all of this training be for naught?* But I now realize that the better our characters are, the closer we are to God, the better we will be able to face the challenges life is sure to bring to us (whether this includes the official "day of trouble" or not), and the better we will be able to assist others. This is truly something worth training for.

Passages to consider: *Romans 5:3-5; James 1:2-4.*

17. You Will Enlarge My Heart

In the act of running there is an instant in each stride in which neither foot is on the ground. For me that instant is getting smaller and smaller, but if a business card can fit between feet and ground during a split second of the stride, I am still running, flying. And as long as I can do that, I tell myself, I will not feel old.

Hey! I was just looking out my office window and saw a professor of a certain age, books to chest, running down the sidewalk. I didn't know she could still run. Still young! Amazing.

I love to run—despite being a runner of very modest ability. They have an official category for me (runners 190 pounds and over): Clydesdale. Ouch. In fact, the horse thing and my lack of speed go way back to second or third grade when we played a tag-type game of pretending that we were horses, chasing each other around the playground. I saw right then that I had more ability in my mouth than my hooves.

A few years later, watching the class dragsters such as Karlen Bailie burning through the 50-yard dash in Presidential Fitness times, I knew that I'd never go that fast without wheels. In the cross-country training section of our eighth-grade physical education, I finished third or fourth from the last of the guys and felt a real sense of accomplishment. When, in 1996, I ran the Chicago Marathon, my goal was to beat Oprah's time (in the Marine Corps Marathon). I did—take that, Steadman!—though I couldn't match my wife, Lilia. Which is just fine, because I married a real runner.

My competitive lowlights occurred in Argentina. In 1995 our family spent seven months at River Plate University, where my wife and I taught English. With no car, television, or committee meetings I had a lot of time on my feet, and I began running more and more.

I thought about training for the Adidas Marathon in Buenos Aires. Meanwhile, there was a 10K race in Nogoya, about an hour away from the school. I was a little surprised when I got there to see only 43 entrants, including Lilia (the only female entrant) and me—in a comparable U.S. race there would have been a few hundred. As I watched the other contestants warming up, I didn't think the competition looked too tough: a dozen or so young guys, one of whom would presumably win the race, and a bunch of middle-aged men. Hey, I might finish in the top third. I fantasized about being able to see the winner finish if, say, there was a mile-long straightaway to the tape.

I knew there were at least a couple people I should beat. There was Marianski, the local shoemaker, a friendly man in his late 50s, I suppose, who a few years earlier had been so hobbled by the constant stooping required of his craft that he could barely walk, much less run. True, he had made remarkable progress since then, but I was not a recovering cobbler. I also thought that, with my extra training, I could give Lilia a run for her money.

The gun sounded. About yard 200 my baseball cap blew off, and I hesitated for a split second. I stopped to pick it up, and suddenly I was at the back of the pack. By mile four I had long given up on finishing in the top third—how did those middle-aged guys run so fast? To be completely forthright, I was running last. But Marianski and my wife were only a hundred yards ahead. I ratcheted up my pace in the next half mile and passed them. After a heady minute running 10 yards ahead of them, I unratcheted. Last again. *Please God*, I pleaded. *I know I'm slow, but is it necessary for my character development that I finish absolutely dead stinking last in a race?* The answer came swiftly.

Shortly after mile five, I rounded a corner and saw a silver-haired man a couple hundred yards ahead—the sacrificial lamb who would allow me to finish "not last." I surged; I passed him; the finish line came into view. I finished at least 50 yards ahead. He panted across the line and shook my hand, and we congratulated each other. Then he told me of his recent Achilles tendon surgery, and about how pleased he was to finally run again. God may still be laughing about my comeuppance in that one.

Another character-building moment occurred in front of thousands at the Adidas Marathon. Simultaneous with the marathon was a 10K race, for which I opted. Serious racers need a game plan, and mine was to hold back my speed until I passed kilometer eight, then burn the jets to the finish line. Everything was going well. I was on pace, accelerating nicely at kilometer nine, turning the corner, looking for the big white "finish line" banner. It was nowhere in sight. We ran on for another couple of minutes. Nothing. The needle was on empty. I saw the long stream of thousands of runners making a wide circle around a park, but no finish line.

I had to get out of the current or be trampled. I stood to the side, bent over. Runners ran by shouting encouragement—"Get a move on, 'flaco.'" After another minute or two I followed their advice and jogged slowly another five minutes to the finish line. It was a 12-kilometer race advertised as a 10K. No wonder their national economy is in trouble! Oh well. I'm still running and therefore, by my private definition, still young.

I love how the apostle Paul compares key points of the Christian life to training for and running a race: "Let us run with endurance the race that is set before us"—even if it's longer or more difficult than we bargained for (Hebrews 12:1). I think back to what got me interested in running a marathon in the first place. I tagged along with Lilia, who was running the 1994 Chicago Marathon. The finish that year wound around one last curve and turned into Grant Park. There was a huge digital time clock, grandstands along the last hundred yards, a helicopter overhead, thousands of cheering people. *I don't know about the first 26 miles*, I thought to myself, *but it would sure be fun to run the last .2 miles of a marathon.* It was partly thinking of that last .2 miles that kept me more or less on my training schedule. I wanted to have the experience of running between the grandstands, crossing the finish line.

The marathon itself was a fantastic experience. To be one of 20,000 people gathered to run 26 miles together is mind-boggling. To hear the *slap, slap, slap* of thousands of sneakered feet all around you is awe-inspiring. I learned some things about values during the race. Even though I am not one to relieve myself in semipublic, I dutifully joined about 50 other males who headed for nearby trees at Lincoln Park, about mile six. Under certain conditions, the rules change. Lilia waited at mile 17 to cheer me on. When I saw her, I pulled off my wristwatch and gave it to her—I didn't want to carry the extra ounce or two seven more miles if I didn't have to. The rules change.

Finally, I turned the last corner and saw the finish line. My joints were weary, but joy surged through me. I crossed the finish line and felt love for all the world, that each of the other runners was my brother or sister. I hugged the woman who hung a "finishers" medal around my neck, and I probably had tears in my eyes. As I later told others, it was a little foretaste of what it will be like to finally arrive in heaven, to join the other celebrants at Jesus' feet. As Christians, we are running for an incorruptible crown that all who complete the course may claim (1 Corinthians 9:24–27); we can look forward to saying with Paul, "I have finished my course" (2 Timothy 4:7).

But perhaps my favorite running text, after Isaiah 40:31—"they will run and not grow weary" (NIV)—is Psalm 119:32, which reads, "I shall run the way of Your commandments, for You will enlarge my heart."

Run and not grow weary? An enlarged and more efficient heart? That's great news—for runners, for Christians, and for Clydesdales who are both.

18. *Hogan*

I recently reread Curt Sampson's interesting biography of golfing great Ben Hogan (*Hogan*, Rutledge Hill Press, 1996). Hogan, who won four U. S. Opens and the minislam of 1953 with the Masters, U. S. Open, and British Open (the one time he played in the event), is considered to be one of the best golfers of the past century. He stood for perfection, especially on full shots, and was known for inventing the modern routine of diligent practice. "There isn't enough daylight in any one day to practice all the shots you need to," he used to say.

Sampson observes that Hogan's practice obsession "helped make him a genius, but it didn't make him happy." As I thought about Hogan and his career, I tried weighing the good and bad sides of his obsession with the golf swing. He could hit one beautiful shot after another, with stunning precision. His shagger (a boy with a baseball mitt) would stand at the other end of the driving range, catching ball after ball without moving. He won many great golf tournaments. He founded a very successful business making golf clubs.

But Hogan's life demonstrates what Solomon discovered long before. That preeminent success in any earthly endeavor is not enough to satisfy the human spirit. Solomon, in addition to being the wisest man in the world, was also one of the wealthiest. In chapter 2 of Ecclesiastes he demonstrates what it is possible for a man with creativity and a bottomless checkbook to attain, launching his endeavor with the statement, "Come now, I will test you with pleasure. So enjoy yourself."

Solomon goes on to build better and better houses for himself; then he tries vineyards; he makes gardens and parks, plants all kinds of fruit trees; he buys male and female slaves, flocks and herds; he collects gold and silver, male and female singers; he assembles a massive harem. Materially speaking, Solomon tried it all, and with excellent taste, no doubt. But in the end, as he says, it was futility, or vanity.

Solomon's experience is recounted for our benefit. It shows us that no great accomplishments in the field of art, engineering, or science—purely in and of themselves—are a sufficient purpose for a human life. It shows us that material pleasures—the best food, wine, sexual adventure—are not going to bring lasting happiness.

We need to think more on Solomon's experience, because it's very easy to fall into the trap of believing that if we only had X, or if we only accomplished Y, then we would be happy. In my case, for instance, I can muse, "If I could only get a book of poems published, or get a new Prius to replace my rusted-out Honda, or play a round of golf under par, or play Bottesini's 'Melody in E' beautifully on the double bass for a special music—if only, if only, then I would be truly happy." We all have a list of things we'd like to accomplish, and the very fact that we haven't yet accomplished them makes them seem especially desirable.

I am drawn to the long-term devotion to acquiring technique in a particular craft, the Hogan spirit. Actually, one of my problems is that I'm drawn to this in several crafts! And it's not bad to want to be good at something, or several things, and to work toward that. We have to remember, however, that we are citizens of two worlds, and if our time and energies are spent out of balance with that concept, then we are out of congruence with reality and will eventually have to pay the price.

What are you doing, today, to invest in that second world? What a shame it would be to win the U. S. Open and not even qualify for the Holy City Invitational.

Passage to consider: *Matthew 16:26.*

19. *People* Magazine

Let's abolish capital punishment and commute existing death sentences to life in prison reading *People*. Of course, we would have to find a way to get this change past the Eighth Amendment, which forbids cruel and unusual punishment, but it's worth a try. The latest issue promises to tell me about Beyoncé's new body. What could possibly make Beyoncé's new or old body of any interest to any rational person, I wonder, but since we're reading *People* in the first place (you're reading it over my shoulder), I guess rationality is hardly relevant.

Flipping to the center of the magazine, we see five pictures of Beyoncé, each from a different year, to show how she has slimmed down from her "bootylicious" period to now. According to the people.com poll, 82 percent of her fans "love her slimmer," while 18 percent "prefer her curvy." Folks, this is the nutritional equivalent to opening our mouths and pouring in a pint of corn oil. If we do this another 10 minutes, our brain waves may flatten forever.

What is it that leads people to buy *People*, to plunk down the price of a decent ice-cream cone for pictures and gossip about celebrities? For many, I fear, it must be a terrible feeling of personal insignificance that, paradoxically, leads a person to latch on to someone "significant." What is a celebrity but the (usually) messed-up version of society stamping "significant" on a person? A celebrity is someone covered by the news media, someone whom paparazzi stake out, someone who sits on the couch across from Oprah and talks about her new movie. A celebrity, by this definition, is someone who matters. And you, noncelebrity reader (and I), do not matter, except as a fan of these valuable celebrities.

127

How would it be if, instead of reading *People* (or should I say looking at *People*, since there's not much to read) for a half hour each week, we tried to make a connection with real people? Such as making a special card for our mom's birthday (something I need to do this afternoon), chatting with the neighbor out mowing his lawn, calling our grandparents just to say hello. As Christians, it should matter very little to us who are the popular celebrities of the hour; the personal relationships we foster, however, can make a difference for eternity.

This topic brings to mind Ellen White's well-known quote from *The Ministry of Healing*: "Christ's method alone will give true success in reaching the people. The Savior mingled with men as one who desired their good. He showed His sympathy for them, ministered to their needs, and won their confidence. Then He bade them 'Follow me'" (p. 143).

Each of us has a responsibility to mingle among people as one who desires their good. This is not just a duty; it's a privilege. *People* promises to fulfill our cravings to get close to important people, but what it provides in the end is a bit of fluff about people we will most likely never meet. Meanwhile, there are fascinating people all around us whom we can meet, get to know in a significant way, and, by God's grace, have a positive impact on their lives. Forget *People*; remember people.

And pray that you don't get convicted of a capital crime in my new regime.

Passage to consider: *Philippians 2:1-4.*

20. *Waco*

The documentary *Waco: The Rules of Engagement* (1997) presents a mosaic of archival footage about the Waco, Texas, tragedy that extended from February 1993, when four ATF agents (from the Bureau of Alcohol, Tobacco, and Firearms) were shot and killed in a raid on the Branch Davidian complex, until April 19, 1993, when more than 70 remaining Davidians were killed by bullets and/or flames.

Naturally, as a Seventh-day Adventist, I wonder about the Davidians. How many of them, including their leader, David Koresh, were former SDAs? How were they like and unlike Adventists? How were they like and unlike me? Seen in the surviving videotapes, many of them seem like decent people, truth-seekers who were willing to go against the mass of society in pursuit of something they thought to be right. On the other hand, there are some obvious differences in (some of) their attitudes toward firearms and family relations.

I was also impressed with the difficulty of arriving at the truth in the face of conflicting testimony. For instance, certain experts in the interpretation of "forward looking infrared" (FLIR) footage taken by an FBI surveillance team assert that the footage conclusively shows automatic weapons firing into the doorway of an area where the Davidians could have escaped the conflagration of April 19, the implication being that the FBI deliberately forced them to die. On the other hand, the FBI states that no such firing occurred, and other experts conclude that the "hot spots" in the footage indicate reflections of the sun. Whom do you believe?

But perhaps the most relevant point, for this book, is that people tend to fear other people who seem different, and in many cases such a fear is magnified far out of proportion to the threat actually posed. This fear can lead to all kinds of unwarranted and unfair actions against those "different" people. Next time "those people" might be Middle Easterners—or people who aren't Middle Easterners but are mistaken for them. It might be gays. It might be Hutus or Tutsis (see the section on *Left to Tell*). It might even be Adventists. After all, they have some pretty strange beliefs, don't they?

Mary Zeiss, in an article for *The Chronicle of Higher Education*, comments that "it may be that what makes religious groups like the Branch Davidians especially threatening from a more 'mainstream' point of view is their sheer devotion to a life-altering, and explicitly countercultural, message. Most Americans balk at that much commitment . . ."

As an Adventist, I do believe that we have a message that is countercultural; in many ways we need to think differently from the mass of our society. And we need to be committed to our message. The issue isn't whether our message will be popular; it's "Is it true, and if so, how can I share it effectively?"

Meanwhile, may we daily ask God for His Spirit to guide us in the way we treat others, as individuals and groups, and may we remember that the basis of His character is love.

Passage to Consider: Matthew 7:12; Matthew 28:19, 20.

21. Aron Ralston

Under what circumstances would you deliberately break your arm?

Probably not under any circumstances that immediately come to mind. Aron Ralston, however, got into a mess in which he was thrilled to discover that he could break his arm, and immediately proceeded to do so. His reaction? He was "sweating and euphoric," "overcome with . . . excitement" (*Between a Rock and a Hard Place*, p. 280).

Ralston, as you may remember, is the outdoor adventurer who, in April of 2003, while solo exploring in a remote Utah canyon, got his arm pinned between an 800-pound boulder and a rock wall. As he had told no one where he was going (let's learn the lesson here), no one knew where to look for him, and after six days of hanging on, Ralston was ready, eager actually, to break his arm in order to make it possible for him to amputate the pinned and dead part of himself so that he could be free.

Ralston's actions for self-preservation captivated national attention. It was fascinating for millions of people who couldn't imagine cutting off their arms to examine the story of someone who did. The story reminded me of one of Christ's "hard sayings," because it literalizes a text we tend to view figuratively: "If your hand or your foot causes you to stumble, cut it off and throw it from you; it is better for you to enter life crippled or lame, than to have two hands or two feet and be cast into the eternal fire" (Matthew 18:8).

The hand is one of the most marvelous of the many marvelous mechanisms of our bodies. When you think of the skill it can develop for the piano, the guitar, a golf club, a paintbrush, typing—just holding a spoon and being able to raise muesli with fresh blueberries to your mouth is a pretty amazing and worthwhile action. Even so, if attachment to it prohibits survival, the hand is dispensable. I would guess that to the extent Aron Ralston is admired, it is because he recognized this and took the decisive action called for by the situation.

Thankfully, none of us are likely to end up in Ralston's exact situation. However, if his life was threatened by an 800-pound boulder, can we feel any better when we are pursued by Satan, who is described as a roaring lion seeking someone to devour (1 Peter 5:8)? The most likely reason for the assertions Christ made in Matthew 18:8, 9 (and parallel texts) is that Christians will come up against temptations that seem as impossible to overcome as would be cutting off your hand or plucking out your eye. But that's stating it in the negative.

Turning it around to the positive, look at the parables of the pearl of great price and the treasure hidden in the field (Matthew 13). Both the one who finds the pearl and the one who finds the hidden treasure are willing, probably even "sweating and euphoric," to sell all that they have so that they can purchase an even greater treasure. One of our country's most cherished values is getting the best deal for the money, putting the right price on a basket of goods. It's no accident that *The Price Is Right* is the longest-running show on TV. What a tragedy it would be, however, if we were able to put the right price on a bottle of Geritol but missed the price on eternal life. I doubt Aron Ralston ever looks back and says, "I wish I would have kept my hand." By God's grace, neither will we.

22. My Way or the "High Way"

In 1969 Paul Anka composed a song, "My Way," written for and most closely associated with Frank Sinatra, although it has since been recorded by dozens of other singers from Aretha Franklin to Julio Iglesias. Indeed, the ubiquity of the song undercuts its message of unique personal identity—but that's another story. In its common usage, "my way or the highway" means that you do things my way or you get out of here, travel on down the highway. But I am using "high way" as two words, and contrasting the "My Way" philosophy to the higher way, or "High Way" proposed by God's Word. Let's look at the lyrics of "My Way."

The dramatic situation of the song is quite interesting. It's written as a philosophical looking back at life, a review of a life lived and the wisdom gained from it. Anka reportedly wrote it after hearing that Sinatra was thinking of retiring. The singer (in the song) is facing the final curtain—retirement, and eventually death. This is the traditional position from which to look back on the meaning of all that one has seen and done, and to make a statement about it, a statement about which the speaker is "certain." What is he so certain about? What is he going to state so clearly?

Obviously, the song's emotional and philosophical cornerstone is the phrase "my way." I did it my way. This person has traveled extensively, loved, laughed, and cried, but the most important thing is that he did these things *his* way. The phrase "my way" appears five times, each time as the culmination of a verse, with "my way" being the final triumphant proclamation of the song. Putting the best face on it, this could be seen as a proclamation of integrity, of doing things as one thinks they ought to be done, regardless of the

131

(presumably) officious interference of others. But given the frequency and positioning of the phrase, it seems reasonable to say that doing things *his way* is the primary value for the speaker.

This is obviously a big problem for the Christian—or for anybody living in a social context. How about conducting a church-sponsored marriage retreat for which "My Way" is the theme song? How about "My Way" as an inspirational song for the next round of meetings between the Israelis and Palestinians? It's not hard to see how a "My Way" philosophy, taken with any seriousness, could be incredibly destructive in any number of situations.

The "My Way" philosophy couldn't be in more stark contrast to Christian philosophy, which is based on seeking to understand and act on God's will for our lives. "Thy word is a lamp unto my feet, and a light unto my path," says the psalmist (Psalm 119:105). "Thy will be done" is part of the Lord's Prayer (Luke 11:2, KJV). Jesus advises us that those who enter heaven will be those who do "the will of My Father who is in heaven" (Matthew 7:21). Jesus lived for the benefit of others at great personal cost and self-sacrifice, not to seek His own will. The culmination of this attitude might be His request, in the Garden of Gethsemane, that His Father remove "this cup" from Him, which ends with "not My will, but Yours be done" (Luke 22:42). In short, there is a distinct difference between "my way" and the "High Way."

Some people, including myself in weaker moments, get stalled from the idea of giving up my way, fearing that we will become brainless puppets in the hands of a manipulating God, with no character or personality of our own. "My way," in this case, seems like the only way to preserve our individuality. Before I get too far down this track, however, I am reminded that God created us to be free individuals; He has shown tremendous restraint in allowing us to exercise our free will, even when it leads to bad choices, hurtful choices, to ourselves and others. It would be self-contradictory for a god who has gone so far to grant and preserve our freedom to want us to be automatons. Rather, I believe, He wants us to reach our fullest and most creative individuality, which we can do only as we seek His will. And in fact, when I think of biblical heroes such as Abraham, Moses, Daniel, Queen Esther, Rahab, Peter, and Paul, I hardly think of brainless automatons, but some of the most distinct personalities recorded in literature. In short, "my way" leads to a deformed, degraded version of the self. But the "High Way" leads to the best, most interesting, and creative self we could be.

Let's turn from "my way" to another phrase in the song: "my friend." The song is sung to someone, a nameless and featureless friend, mentioned in its third line. It's all well and good to go around singing "my way," but what's the point if no one else can hear you, and best of all, a friend? What can we learn about personal relationships from the song? Well, the singer has loved, laughed, and cried, presumably all in a social context. The singer has loved, but has no lover. The singer alludes to the friend in the stanza in which he faces life's problems—"when I bit off more than I could chew," as the lyrics have it. However, there's no implication that the friend was able to help or intervene, because the singer remains supremely self-sufficient. "But through it all," he boasts, "when there was doubt, I ate it up and spit it out," and there we are tobogganing down the hill to another exclamation of "my way." The sad conclusion is that "my way" thinking is based on the illusion (it appears to me) that the individual self against the world is the ultimate reality. If we look just a little at Sinatra's personal life, it's not hard to see the results of "my way" thinking.

As quaint as it may seem today, two months before his first marriage Sinatra was arrested on a morals charge for having an affair with a married woman. He was married four times—to Nancy Barbato, Ava Gardner (called the most beautiful woman in the world), Mia Farrow, and Barbara Marx. He had affairs too numerous to mention; however, none of these relationships satisfied him. His daughter Tina made an interesting comment in regard to his affair with Ava Gardner, which began while he was married to Barbato. In *My Father's Daughter* Tina writes that her father "didn't understand that [Ava Gardner] could never replace the happiness he had forfeited at home. He was a man who all his life looked outside for what was missing inside" (p. 22).

Later, when his daughters were having their own romantic liaisons and father Sinatra tried to reprimand them, they pointed to his record, to which he gave the classic lame answer, "You'll do as I say, not as I do." Sadly, both Sinatra daughters married and divorced at an early age, and Nancy Sinatra's signature song, "These Boots Are Made for Walkin'," fits right in with this picture of negative relationships, with the final phrase forecasting the disintegration of two lovers: "one of these days these boots are gonna walk all over you." "My way" thinking is corrosive to partnerships.

But perhaps the most perceptive comment on the "my way" philosophy was made by Sinatra himself, as reported by Tina: "There's nothing worse . . . than

133

being an old swinger" (p. 145). Here Sinatra illustrates the remorse of one who has been hoodwinked by the world's ways. To some minds, nothing could seem more appealing than being a young swinger, glamorous, desirable and desiring, enjoying the flesh to its fullest, committed to nothing but your own pleasure. But then what happens? You have to live with the regrets that accrue from years of unfaithfulness, years of putting pleasure before principle, and the pleasure itself turns to ashes in the mouth as it always does when it's put before principle. Nothing worse than being an old swinger.

Let's look at one last section of the song, the last stanza, in which the speaker claims that a real man says "the things he truly feels, and not the words of one who kneels." In the mind of the world, the things one truly feels must be the opposite of the words of one who is kneeling, whereas for the Christian, the words of one who kneels must be the deepest and most profound expression of feeling. The reverence and submission implied by kneeling is wholly appropriate before God and carries no shame. Rather, it is shameful to cling to a pride that loathes to kneel before anyone, even God. "The fear of the Lord is the beginning of wisdom, and the knowledge of the Holy One is understanding" (Proverbs 9:10). The "my way" philosophy refuses to kneel. The "High Way" philosophy requires kneeling on a regular basis.

In fact, I would submit that it is only through a lot of kneeling, or praying, that an individual can move from "my way" to the "High Way." It was, presumably, Jesus' time alone with His heavenly Father that allowed Him to say "not My will but Yours." It is that daily connection with God, the moment by moment dependence, that allows us to rise above "my way" to a better way.

A final point about "My Way" thinking. "My Way" thinking sees the individual self as the most important entity. The "High Way" is about relationships—first, about our relationship with God, but also about our relationship with others. The individual is always seen in a theological and social context. As we believe in the Trinity, we believe that God created humans in His image, to live in a social context, with Him and with each other. In this context, "my way" can never be the most important value; rather, it is a destructive value, and needs to be recognized as such. God gives us the opportunity to make a choice. We can live the "High Way," seeking to know God in personal friendship, enjoying the blessed opportunity to build up those around us, or we can live "my way," seeking our selfish purposes, and living out a degrading parody of the beautiful relationships God wants for us.

Joshua 24:15 calls us to "Choose you this day whom ye will serve" (KJV). Let's turn away from "my way" and follow the "High Way."

23. *Esperanza*

Esperanza means "hope," a nugget I picked up many years ago while pursuing my future wife, an Argentinian. It was a word I needed then—and a word I need now as I look around the sanctuary on the last Friday night of our church's five-week evangelistic effort.

The team is ready to go. The greeters are out in the lobby, supplied with name tags and registration cards. Lillis and the prayer warriors are on their knees on the other side of the one-way window to the parents' room. Terry and the camera crew are rolling with the DVD production. Dan and Lathan have checked the PowerPoint projection. John is sitting at the sound board. Anita and Julia and the Pathfinders have the child care under control. Bob is here, ready to wait an hour and a half to sing the closing song. Ken and Jeremiah, the ministerial interns, sit with their wives, ready to come forward and answer questions at the close of the meeting. Peter slides in beside me after playing 20 minutes of meditational music on the piano. All told, there is a crew of about 40 members, including those of us forming part of the congregation. And one visitor.

I don't know whether to laugh or cry. Our church invested considerable time and money to send invitations to the community; there were door-to-door visitations; we have all this apparatus in place. But we're not merely counting on our human efforts: we're praying and asking God to lead in everything. And we have just one, o-n-e candidate for baptism! Where, O Lord, are the fields of grain, ready for harvest?

Up until last weekend an elderly couple attended, sitting right up in front and taking notes, but they dropped out. A few others came early on and stopped. If this were a college class, the administration would have closed it a long time ago and redeployed the teacher. I hope the pastor is not depressed.

On the other hand, there are many things to accept with gratitude. I have been blessed by going over Bible prophecies again, and impressed that I need to know God's Word more deeply. It has been a tremendous gift to see the church youth incorporated into the team as camera operators, puppeteers, and child supervisors. And for each night's meeting, other youth have given the introductions from a prepared script. Although it has put a burden on our already-full schedules, these meetings have drawn many of us in the congregation closer together in working for the Lord. And there is that one woman.

A few nights ago the pastor alluded to the story of Elisha at Dothan (2 Kings 6). You remember how Elisha's servant was overwhelmed with the sight of the Syrian army surrounding the city until Elisha asked God to open the servant's eyes. Then he saw the hosts of God's army, and his perspective completely changed.

My eyes are not fully opened yet to see things as Elisha and his servant saw them, but I can see reason for hope. Our visitor is very enthusiastic about the message. She has been passing on the DVDs to her husband and one of her friends. In a few weeks she will be revisiting her native Colombia, seeing family and friends, no doubt sharing the good news she loves. Who knows where the ripples will stop? Who knows the extent to which God can use these meetings? For adults. For our church youth. For our visitor. For her friends and family. Who knows? Her name, I should tell you, is Esperanza.

Passage to consider: Luke 15.

24. Why I Believe in God

We usually leave this topic to theologians or people such as Ben Carson—for good reason, I find, as I erase sentence after sentence of my draft. I'm afraid of embarrassing God (or more likely myself) by my inadequate defense. On the other hand, Christians should be able to articulate their reasons for faith, and it's a wonderful privilege to say good things about God, so here goes . . .

Heritage. I was raised in a religious home, and although over a period of 48 years I have had periods of serious doubt about the existence and benevolence of God, my upbringing has made taking God into account a reflexive action. This, in itself, has not made me a believer, but it has forced me to be very aware of making a conscious choice in the matter.

The Bible. As an English teacher I have read a lot of books, but nothing like this book. It boggles my mind that the writing of it stretches nearly 2,000 years, that it was written by many different authors, yet fits together. The idea of putting a book like this together and pulling it off is, in my scale of probability, much more like God than Random House. Also, many parts of it, such as the Ten Commandments; the stories of Noah, Abraham, Joseph, Esther,

136

Ruth, David; the Great Commandment—and I could go on and on—seem beyond human wisdom, yet powerfully attractive.

The Life of Jesus. As an extension of the previous section, I find Jesus' life and character to be a compelling reason—perhaps the most compelling reason—to believe in the existence and benevolence of God. Jesus, to my eyes, does not at all seem to be a literary character in the sense that Ulysses is, or explainable as a historical human. The way His thinking both diverges from that of His time (as in His treatment of women, distinction between true religion and false, and so forth) and natural human tendencies, yet seems more sane and right the longer you look at it, is His certificate of authenticity. I don't think Jesus could be made up. I think He "was."

Science/Nature. I look out my window and see the seasons change. I read the accounts of the latest Faith and Science Conference in Denver in the *Adventist Review* and *Spectrum Online*. I have the extraordinary experience of inhabiting a human body; an ongoing experience of the outside world through this body; and a limited book knowledge of science/faith issues.

Although an incredible number of things about the human body can be explained by science (thankfully), I have a hard time believing nonsupernatural theories about the origin of life. On the other hand, I have no adequate knowledge base from which to refute various tenets of evolution, such as the long age of the Earth. Nor does this lack of certainty keep me awake.

I think I understand the basic idea of "intelligent design" (ID), and it appeals to my sense of logic. Nevertheless, I have to take the proofs of ID on faith. In short, "book science" has plenty to say for and against the existence of God. I have only a layperson's knowledge here, but find no deeply disturbing "facts" that counter my belief, nor do I have any irrefutable proofs of God's existence.

As I look around the earth, humans seem to be a very distinctly different class of "animals" from any other, and to me it seems more likely that this is a result of a specific act of creation than an outgrowth of evolution. I don't expect to persuade a lot of people with this modest idea. I'm just saying that it appeals to me.

Likewise, being able to think a thought such as *wiggle your toes* and make that instantly happen at the other end of the body from the command center seems to me so miraculous a process as to warrant a belief in God's existence. Whitman's line about a mouse being enough to stagger sextillions of infidels comes to mind—although plenty of infidels still seem to be standing upright.

People I Admire. Most of the people I have deeply admired over the years have been committed Christians. "Great people" who are living for only this life seem, to my way of thinking, to be a contradiction in terms. And if God exists, they definitely are. Although I'm giving short space to this reason, it is one of the most important for me.

Intuition. Believing in God feels right to me. Is this because religion is the opiate of the people, or because God planted something in me that responds to Him? In either case, my intuition leans toward God. Furthermore, it seems right to me to consider all humans on this planet as my brothers and sisters, rather than as competitors in a survival of the fittest. This concept is not unique to a Christian perspective, but it is central to it and not natural to a materialist perspective.

Morality. I have a hard time believing in an objective standard of morality without believing in God. I have a hard time believing the scientific explanations of altruism, unselfishness, compassion. Yes, it is "incredible" to contemplate the love of God, but that very magnificence leads me to believe that it comes from God, not humans.

Changed Lives. The apostle Paul, Nicky Cruz, Doug Batchelor, John Newton, Hudson Taylor, Mary Magdalene. History is replete with people whose lives were dramatically changed by getting to know God. There's a lot of evidence that He makes an all-important difference in many people's attitudes, perceptions, and sense of purpose.

Tolerance for Open Questions. There are many things I don't have answers for. Free will goes a certain distance in explaining the problem of pain, but I still have questions in that area. I'm not sure how the Pentateuch was composed. I believe that intercessory prayer is a good thing and that something happens when such prayers are offered, but there are many things about it that I don't understand. I am with C. S. Lewis in believing that we will have a lot of surprises when we get to heaven about ideas we were pretty sure of on earth.

Well, there's a draft of my reasons. What would your draft look like?

25. Rubber

A book that starts with gold and ends with rubber—talk about devaluation. But wait a second. Have anything rubber around you? I'm wearing rubber-soled shoes, have rubber in the seal of my wristwatch, rubber on the tires on my bike and car, rubber on the antenna of the cordless phone. Without rubber, my favorite sport, golf, would consist of whacking a hard pellet short distances along the ground—in other words, hockey. Just kidding, dear Canadian reader, and yes, I do know that the puck is made out of rubber.

I have to confess that I mostly took rubber for granted until I listened to the audiobook of *Noble Obsession* (2002), by Charles Slack, which tells the fascinating story of Charles Goodyear and the development of the world's rubber industry. Rubber had been known to Europeans since Columbus's second voyage, during the 1490s, and, of course, was known to the natives of the Americas long before that. In some respects, rubber seemed to be a miracle compound. It had wonderful properties not shared (in combination) by any other substance. As Slack notes, it was pliant, waterproof, airtight, moldable, and did not conduct electricity (p. 1). "Rubber became the great shock absorber of the industrial age" (p. 2). But that was in the last half of the nineteenth century.

During the first half of the century, despite its wonderful properties, rubber was not widely used. There were, of course, lots of rubber erasers around, rubber shoes, and rubber raincoats, but rubber did not catch on more widely because of its fatal flaw. Prior to Goodyear's discovery of vulcanization in 1839—and most of another decade spent in perfecting the process—rubber lost its desirable properties in extreme temperatures, either hot or cold. In heat, rubber started to melt, not to mention that it gave off a disgusting smell. In cold, rubber lost its pliability, and cracked. Not surprisingly, customers did not take kindly to goods that performed well only within an ideal range of temperatures, and many investors in the early rubber industry saw their investments turn to total losses as rubber's wonderful properties were undermined by its fatal flaw.

As I listened to the story of rubber, I couldn't help thinking that humans are a lot like rubber: a combination of wonderful properties, including advanced language skills, incredible development in music, the ability to plan for the future, compassion, the ability to solve a Rubik's Cube (not me, but true for some humans). However, like prevulcanized rubber, we have a fatal flaw, akin to melting in heat and cracking in cold. The human spirit under duress, like rubber, loses its elasticity and can become of no more use than a stinking pile of goo or a cracked plate.

Fortunately, God has a process that, like what vulcanization does for rubber, makes a wonderful transformation of human weakness. Paul tells us that "the Spirit also helps our weakness" (Romans 8:26) and that God's power "is perfected in [human] weakness" (2 Corinthians 12:9); that he "can do all things through [Christ] who strengthens me" (Philippians 4:13); that God "will supply all [our] needs according to His riches in glory in Christ Jesus" (Philippians 4:19). We need God's transforming power for our talents to be maximized, for our work to be worthwhile, for anything we do to be of lasting value.

Vulcanized rubber changed the world; so can human beings who submit themselves to God's transforming power.

Passage to consider: *John 15:1-5.*

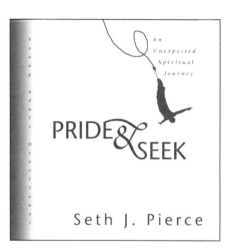

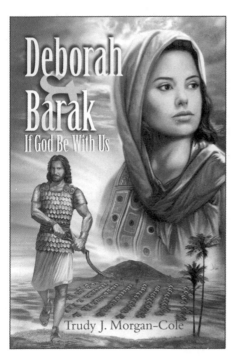